Inheritance Tax Planning Handbook: 2017

Lee J Hadnum

IMPORTANT LEGAL NOTICES:

WealthProtectionReportTM
TAX GUIDE - "Inheritance Tax Planning Handbook"

Published by:
WealthProtectionReport.co.uk
Email: sales@wealthprotectionreport.co.uk

Third Edition: February 2017

Copyright

Trademarks

DISCLAIMER

1. Please note that this tax guide is intended as general guidance only for individual readers and does NOT constitute accountancy, tax, legal, investment or other professional advice. WealthProtectionReport and the author accept no responsibility or liability for loss which may arise from reliance on information contained in this tax guide.

2. Please note that tax legislation, the law and practices by government and regulatory authorities (for example, HM Revenue and Customs) are constantly changing and the information contained in this tax guide is only correct as at the date of publication. We therefore recommend that for accountancy, tax, investment or other professional advice, you consult a suitably qualified accountant, tax specialist, independent financial adviser, or other professional adviser. Please also note that your personal circumstances may vary from the general examples given in this tax guide and your professional adviser will be able to give specific advice based on your personal circumstances.

3. This tax guide covers UK taxation mainly and any references to 'tax' or 'taxation' in this tax guide, unless the contrary is expressly stated, are to UK taxation only. Please note that references to the 'UK' do not include the Channel Islands or the Isle of Man. Addressing all foreign tax implications is beyond the scope of this tax guide.

4. Whilst in an effort to be helpful, this tax guide may refer to general guidance on matters other than UK taxation, WealthProtectionReport and the author are not experts in these matters and do not accept any responsibility or liability for loss which may arise from reliance on such information contained in this tax guide.

CONTENTS

ABOUT THE AUTHOR

Lee Hadnum LLB ACA CTA is a UK tax specialist. He is a Chartered Accountant and Chartered Tax Adviser and is the Editor of the popular tax planning website:

www.wealthprotectionreport.co.uk

You can e-mail Lee directly at:

Lee@wealthprotectionreport.co.uk with tax planning questions

Members of www.wealthprotectionreport.co.uk can access thousands of articles and can download all of Lee's tax books (50+ books at 1 January 2016) completely free of charge.

Lee is the author of a number of best selling tax planning books including:

- **Tax Planning Techniques Of The Rich & Famous** - Essential reading for anyone who wants to use the same tax planning techniques as the most successful Entrepreneurs, large corporations and celebrities

- **The Worlds Best Tax Havens** – 220 page book looking at the worlds best offshore jurisdictions in detail

- **Inheritance Tax Planning Handbook** – Detailed tax planning for anyone looking to reduce inheritance tax.

- **Non Resident & Offshore Tax Planning** – Offshore tax planning for UK residents or anyone looking to purchase UK property or trade in the UK. A comprehensive guide.

- **Tax Planning With Offshore Companies & Trusts: The A-Z Guide** - Detailed analysis of when and how you can use offshore companies and trusts to reduce your UK taxes

- **Tax Planning For Company Owners** – How company owners can reduce income tax, corporation tax and NICs

- **CGT Planning Handbook** – Tax planning for anyone looking to reduce UK capital gains tax

- **Buy To Let Tax Planning** – How property investors can reduce income tax, CGT and inheritance tax

- **Asset Protection Handbook** – Looks at strategies to ringfence your assets in today's increasing litigious climate

- **Working Overseas Guide** – Comprehensive analysis of how you can save tax when working overseas

- **Double Tax Treaty Planning** – How you can use double tax treaties to reduce UK taxes

1. INTRODUCTION

Inheritance tax is a particularly nasty tax as it's a tax on your capital that you've accumulated from your after tax earnings.

It currently applies at 40% on the value of your estate above the nil rate band (currently £325,000). It's not just the assets held at the date of your death, but also assets gifted away (in some cases) up to 14 years before.

In this book we look at some of the top ways you can legally reduce your inheritance tax liability.

There are a number of options and opportunities – from simply giving away assets to setting up a trust or emigrating from the UK completely.

2. SUMMARY OF HOW INHERITANCE TAX APPLIES TO GIFTS

In this chapter we summarise some of the main tax considerations you should bear in mind when making gifts.

Inheritance Tax ("IHT") in a Nutshell

IHT is primarily a death duty, but also to a lesser extent a tax on lifetime gifts.

On death the estate on hand is, subject to various exemptions and reliefs, liable to IHT.

The principal exemption is for assets passing to a surviving spouse or civil partner, these will pass free of IHT. This is subject to the qualification that, if the deceased spouse/civil partner is domiciled in the UK but the survivor is not, generally the exemption is limited to £325,000 on a lifetime basis.

Property passing to charity is also exempt.

The most significant reliefs are for qualifying business or agricultural property (each a subject in itself), at usually 100% of the value, though in some cases just 50%.

We will deal with some of the other exemptions and reliefs in more detail below.

The rate of IHT

Generally, the first £325,000 (the nil-rate band) of the estate is charged at 0%, with the balance at 40%.

Since April 2012, the rate of IHT applied to the estate can also be reduced from 40% to 36% where, in short, 10% of the estate is left to charity. We look at this later in the book.

In addition to your own nil-rate band, under the 'transferable nil-rate band' rule introduced in October 2007, it is possible to utilise any proportion of the nil-rate band which was unused on the first death within a marriage/civil partnership. For example, if a husband leaves his whole estate to his wife on his death, on the wife's death her estate would benefit from her own nil-rate band plus her husband's, giving a total of £650,000.

Calculating the chargeable estate

The important point is that all property owned at death potentially comes within the IHT charge, subject to exemptions or reliefs. Property must be valued on an open market basis, including 'personal chattels' (house contents, personal possessions and so on).

Added to the value of the estate on death (including a share in any jointly held property) will be certain other property, including the value of:

- Certain trusts;
- Most gifts made within 7 years of death (so called 'Potentially Exempt Transfer' which are discussed in further detail below); and
- Any property given away (since 18 March 1986) in which a 'reservation of a benefit' has been made.

We should say for completeness that the above is a very brief summary only and should not be taken as a comprehensive review.

However, on this basis, you should be able to work out roughly what the potential IHT bill might be on your death and, therefore, whether you might like to think about taking some action now to mitigate it.

Capital Gains Tax

There is, generally, no Capital Gains Tax ("CGT") payable on death. That is, any inherent gain (or indeed loss) in an asset (for example, an investment) is effectively 'washed', so that the beneficiaries inherit the asset at market value at death for CGT purposes.

How do you stand?

If, on perhaps a 'back of the envelope' calculation, you estimate that a significant IHT liability will arise and you would rather benefit your family than the Chancellor of the Exchequer, you might like to consider some options for lifetime giving. The aim would be to reduce the size of the potentially chargeable estate on death.

Other options, outside of making lifetime gifts, for mitigation might include either acquiring (or enhancing the value of) property attracting agricultural or business property relief or indeed writing in trust life policies not already in trust.

Lifetime Giving

CGT

While it might seem a bit odd to start with CGT, you should remember that a gift is just as much a disposal as is a sale. Cash, is not a chargeable asset, nor indeed normally is one's only or main residence. There are also one or two further small exemptions.

Potentially exempt transfers ("PETs")

A gift to an individual (or to a trust for a disabled person) where the donor lives for seven years after making the gift is exempt. If death occurs within seven years, any such gifts have first call on the nil-rate band (in the order they were made). Where the gift(s) exceeds the nil rate band IHT will be payable at the normal rates (subject to tapering relief in certain cases).

Any appreciation in value between the date of gift and the date of death within seven years effectively escapes IHT so far as the donor is concerned. The corollary is that any fall in value is not relieved, as the chargeable value is that at the date of the gift -- unless the gift exceeds the nil-rate band, in which case an election can be made to substitute the lower value at the date of gift.

The spouse/civil partner exemption applies to lifetime gifts just as it does to gifts on death, including the limitation for non-UK domiciled donees.

Before making a PET

When planning to make a sizeable PET, consider whether any chargeable transfers (i.e. a payment into a trust) have been made within the previous seven years; if so, it may be advisable to wait.

And in selecting assets for the PET, favour those that are more likely to appreciate in value --and which do not produce income, which you may not wish to lose.

Ensure that you are not reserving any form of benefit in the gift. If a donor does reserve a benefit (without paying fully for it), the asset will not effectively leave the chargeable estate until such time (if ever) as the benefit ends.

Normally, reservation of benefit is not a problem with gifts between spouses/civil partners, unless the donee is non-UK domiciled for IHT purposes, when issues can arise.

The annual exemption

Gifts of £3,000 in a tax year are exempt. An allowance which is unused in one year can be carried forward for the next year (only).

Assume therefore that you gave £1,000 within this exemption during 2015/16; for 2016/17 you have £3,000 for 2016/17 plus £2,000 carried forward from 2015/16.

Regular use of this exemption is advisable, if you can afford it.

Over a 10 year period you can get £30,000 free of IHT out of your chargeable estate (or £60,000 per married couple/civil partnership), saving at least £12,000 or £24,000 of tax respectively.

The simplest way to use the exemption is to give cash, although you could also make a gift in kind, e.g. a painting worth £3,000. You might chose to pay premiums on a life assurance policy on your life written in trust for your children. Or you could set up or pay into a stakeholder pension for a child or grandchild. You could pay £2,880 net, i.e. within the annual exemption (which represents the maximum contribution of £3,600 gross less 20% basic rate tax). Here you hope that there will be long-term appreciation for the child or grandchild and, which you may consider an advantage, benefits cannot be taken until age 55.

The £250 small gifts exemption

You can make gifts of up to £250 to any one individual in a tax year as exempt, though not in conjunction with the £3,000 annual exemption. This is intended to cover birthday presents, Christmas presents and the like. This exemption is per donee, whereas the annual exemption is per donor.

The normal expenditure out of income exemption

If you have sufficient left from your annual income after paying all 'normal expenditure' (including Income Tax), it is possible to give all or part of the balance away, IHT- exempt. Careful planning and detailed record keeping are required to utilise this exemption fully.

The marriage/civil partnership exemption

When a son or daughter (or step-son or step-daughter) gets married or enters into a civil partnership, a gift will be exempt depending on the relationship between donor and donee:

- £5,000 for parents;
- £2,500 for grandparents; and
- £1,000 for all others.

This gift must be outright, though it can be made into certain types of trust. The gift can be cash or in kind.

The charities exemption

A gift to charity which is made during your lifetime is exempt just as much as on death. One advantage of lifetime gifts is Gift Aid Income Tax relief, both basic rate recovery for the charity and higher rate relief for the donor (with no limit).

If you are considering making a significant lifetime gift to charity (or indeed making a similar gift in your will) it is worthwhile considering establishing your own charitable trust during your lifetime. This way, you are able to remove the assets from your estate (free of tax and, generally, with the benefit of Gift Aid Income Tax relief), whilst being able to shape the grant making policy of the trust during your lifetime.

Other exemptions

There are a variety of other exemptions from IHT, e.g. gifts for national purposes, gifts to employee trusts and so on.

Gifts into trust

Finally, it is important to remember that some lifetime gifts will not be regarded as PETs, and trigger an immediate payment of IHT.

The principal among these are gifts into a trust (other than for a charity or for a qualifying disabled beneficiary). This means that, to the extent the nil-rate band is not available, the gift will attract an immediate IHT charge of 20%, rising to 40% if death follows within seven years.

The big traditional non-tax advantage of gifts into trust is asset protection: any beneficiary will receive only by way of income or capital either what they are entitled to under the settlement or as the trustees determine, that is capital can be preserved in the unfortunate event of personal insolvency.

Matrimonial breakdown is more difficult: a divorce court is not necessarily precluded from treating assets held within a trust as a 'financial resource' of a divorcing beneficiary, in circumstances where the court considers that part of the trust fund is in reality being used (or will be used) for the benefit of that beneficiary -- although it will probably stop short of ordering the trustees to make a distribution to the beneficiary.

3. HOW THE EXEMPTION FOR NORMAL TRANSFERS OF INCOME APPLIES

In inheritance tax exemption that is often overlooked is the exemption for 'normal expenditure out of income'. Where this applies it can lead to amounts paid to family/relative/a trust to be excluded from a deceased's estate when calculating any inheritance tax charge.

In order for payments under the normal expenditure out of income exemption to be exempt, the following conditions must be satisfied:

- the transfer must be made as part of the normal expenditure of the transferor
- it must be made out of his income
- after allowing for all transfers forming part of his normal expenditure, the transferor was left with sufficient income to maintain his usual standard of living.

All three conditions must be satisfied and the onus is on the tax payer to show that they are all satisfied. HMRC accept that it could be that only part of a transfer actually meets the conditions and you'd therefore have a situation where part of a gift was excluded from the estate and the remainder was included.

'Normal expenditure' means that based on the particular transferor, the payment was typical for them. Ideally a regular pattern of payments should be made, or an agreed percentage (eg 10%) of net income would need to be shown to be paid to the recipients.

One way that expenditure could be classed as 'normal' would be for an individual to have assumed a commitment or adopted a firm resolution regarding his future expenditure and thereafter complied with it. There would therefore need to be evidence supporting the regular payments. This could be a simple family agreement indicating payments to be made by (for example) a father to his children.

A common example is where a specific payment is to be made monthly or annually . This could be (for example) payments of £2,808 per tax year into a stakeholder pension for the benefit of a child.

If a regular cash transfer is to be made to a child, a good option would be to consider making any payments under a deed of covenant. This would be likely to satisfy HMRC that a pattern of expenditure will be in place.

In essence the final condition above relates to whether the deceased would have sufficient income to live on after making the transfers in question. His usual standard of living is taken to generally be the standard prevailing at the time of the transfer.

HMRC could therefore look to see details of the net income of the deceased and compare this with the usual costs of living they incur. This can however be a useful way to transfer significant sums over a few tax years without being caught by the 7 year rule.

How much can you give?

There is no limit to the amount you can give away. As a rule of thumb, look at it as a gift of surplus income that would otherwise have been available for saving. Provided the above conditions are met, the entire amount should qualify for immediate IHT exemption.

When should I make the gifts?

There is no strict rule as to when the gifts should be made. However, in order to demonstrate that the income is surplus to your needs, perhaps the better time to make the gifts is towards the end of each tax year when you have a clear idea of your income and (likely) expenditure for that year. Alternatively, if you want to get ahead, set up a monthly or quarterly standing order of a "safe" amount and "top up" at the tax year end.

For how many years should I make the gifts?

Again, there is no strict rule. However, in order to demonstrate that the gifts are being made as part of a settled pattern, it is advisable that you continue to make the gifts over a number of years. Or at least you should demonstrate the intention from the outset to do this.

Much will depend on your circumstances, eg your age and affordability.

Demonstrating a settled pattern of giving comes down to the written evidence. This is crucial in order to reduce the risk of HM Revenue & Customs successfully challenging the effectiveness of the gifts. This also makes the task of administering your estate much easier for your executors and thereby reduces the time and costs of the exercise.

Should I pay the money into a nominated account for my children or grandchildren?

No. Nominated (or designated) accounts are inflexible and can create problems in the future.

For example, when the child reaches the age of 18, they can call on the funds in the account to be paid to them. For obvious reasons, this is likely to be inappropriate: the child will be entitled to spend the money as they wish which, at that age, may well be in a way in which you disapprove.

Even if they do not call on the funds, there are significant disadvantages if the funds are held in a nominated or designated account.

- The funds will be exposed to IHT on the child's death.
- The funds will be exposed to a claim by a divorcing spouse.
- The funds will be exposed to a claim by a creditor.

In short, using a nominated or designated account will not protect the funds and is unlikely to have achieved what you intended.

Protect the gifts: use a trust

These problems can be avoided by using a suitably drafted trust.

Gifts made to a trust have a number of advantages:

- you can act as trustee which will give you control of how the funds are invested and distributed
- the funds (and any growth) will not only escape IHT on your death: they will also escape IHT on your beneficiaries' deaths
- the funds are protected from potential non tax threats such as divorce or the financial vulnerability of the beneficiaries
- if only one of you and your spouse (or civil partner) is making the gifts to the trust, the other of you can benefit from the trust as well as the other beneficiaries (eg your children or grandchildren)
- the structure can be particularly attractive for funding children's education costs and providing funds for them in an IHT efficient way, eg to help them with the purchase of their first property

4. WHEN THE 7 YEAR PERIOD BECOMES A 14 YEAR PERIOD

It's pretty well known that there is a seven year rule for Inheritance tax purposes. So provided you survive for seven years from the date of making most gifts they will be excluded from your estate. Of course if one of the exemptions applies as outlined in the previous chapters you won't have to wait for 7 years.

However, in most other cases the 7 year rule will apply.

This is tremendously useful as a way of reducing the value of your estate, and providing you can keep any CGT chargeable as a result of the transfer to a minimum you could eliminate a substantial chunk of IHT.

Whilst the 7 year rules applies to most non-exempt gifts, if you're considering making any transfers to a trust this seven year rule can be modified, and you can actually end up paying IHT if you die not within seven years, but even within fourteen years.

Transfers to a trust

Transfers to most trusts will be classed as chargeable lifetime transfers ('CLT's). Before March 2006 this only applied to transfers to discretionary trusts, but now after this date transfers to all trusts aside from trusts for a disabled person will be classed as CLT's.

This means that you'll need to be even more concerned with 'time limits' if you're using a trust than previously.

How the seven year rule generally works

Basically when you make a gift it could either be a CLT or a PET ('Potentially Exempt Transfer'). A PET is usually a gift made between individuals.

When you make a CLT you need to assess whether there is any IHT payable at the date of the transfer (irrespective of your future date of death).

To do this you will look at the amount of the nil rate band for that tax year as reduced by any chargeable transfers in the previous seven years (ie CLT's). So if you make a CLT in 2016 you will have a NRB of £325,000. If you made a previous transfer to the trust in 2013 of £100,000 the available nil rate band would £225,000. You'd then compare the available nil rate band with the amount of the current CLT. If the current CLT exceeded the Nil rate band the excess would be taxed at 20%.

When you make a PET, there is no immediate tax charge.

If you died within seven years of making either a PET or a CLT you would then need to also consider the tax position on death. In both cases you would offset the available nil rate band against the transfer to determine whether any excess remained. If there was this would be taxed at 40%.

If you'd previously paid lifetime IHT on a CLT this could be offset against the tax payable on death (ie the 20% difference, although there would be other differences as the NRB when calculating the death tax would be higher than the lifetime tax).

The available nil rate band on death

However the important point to grasp is that when looking at the available nil rate band to offset against a PET that has become chargeable (because you died within seven years of making it) you look at the chargeable transfers made in the previous seven years before that gift (in other words you look back up to 14 years). As a transfers will only be a chargeable transfer if made more than seven years before death where it was a CLT we're mainly looking here at cases where you made a transfer to a trust within 14 years of the date of death.

I appreciate this is confusing so lets run through an example which will hopefully make it much clearer.

Example showing the impact of the 14 year rule

Giles has made the following gifts:

20 June 2007 - £150,000 to a discretionary trust

20 September 2012 - £250,000 to his daughter

Giles dies on 15 November 2017 and has an estate of £500,000.

The Nil Rate Band for 2017/2018 is £325,000.

In terms of Inheritance tax the position is:

- the CLT made on 20 June 2007 was made more than seven years prior to his death and is therefore not subject to IHT.
- the PET made in September 2012 is now chargeable as he has
died within seven years.

As the PET is within the £325,000 nil rate band, no IHT would usually be payable on death.

However, when calculating the IHT due on the PET, the CLT made in the seven years prior to that gift affects the amount of IHT payable:

	£
Nil rate band on death	325,000
Less previous chargeable transfer	150,000
less two annual exemptions	144,000
Nil rate band available for use against PET	181,000

The IHT on the PET would then be calculated as:

Gift in September 2012	250,000
Less 2 annual exemptions	6,000
Less Nil rate band	181,000

Total estate	63,000
IHT @ 40%	25,200
Less taper relief 60%	15,120
IHT payable	10,080

Therefore in this case the CLT that was made more than 10 years before death has resulted in a £10,000 tax charge. This would be payable by the recipient of the gift, in this case his daughter.

The Estate of Giles will not be impacted by this and the tax charge would be be calculated ignoring the earlier CLT transfer. Ie the estate would suffer IHT calculated as:

Estate	500,000
Nil rate band	325,000
Less failed PET in 2011	244,000
Taxable Estate	419,000
IHT @ 40%	167,600

Therefore the net effect of this is that the CLT made more than seven years prior to death reduced the available NRB and therefore can result in tax payable on a later PET. This could apply up to 14 years from the date of death.

5. WHAT TO DO AND WHEN TO AVOID INHERITANCE TAX

You're probably already aware of some inheritance tax planning techniques. The 7 year rule is pretty well known, however in this chapter we look to bring it all together to tell you exactly what you can do and when to avoid inheritance tax.

Life expectancy over 7 years

If you're expecting to live over 7 years you can still make gifts and benefit from the exemption after 7 years.

This means you can transfer cash to your children and potentially save the 40% inheritance tax completely. You'll need to be careful if you're looking to transfer assets such as properties as these would also be subject to capital gains tax on the transfer.

Nevertheless the 7 year exemption applies equally to transfers to trusts as it does to individuals. You could therefore establish a trust and transfer assets within the scope of CGT to this to gain a CGT deferral. We look at this later in the book.

Alternatively you could just raise debt and then gift this to family members. The debt would reduce the value of your estate, but the gift would be excluded from your estate after 7 years.

Life expectancy 2-7 years

As well as the planning outlined below you could consider investing in business property. The main one here will be unquoted shares in trading companies. These will frequently be AIM listed shares and may qualify for 100% business property relief provided you've owned them for at least 2 years.

Making such an investment could therefore eliminate inheritance tax on the investment made.

There are other benefits of such an investment as well. Most notably there's the CGT deferral if you have made any chargeable disposals as well as the 30% income tax credit to reduce your income tax charge.

Life expectancy less than 2 years

In this case you should be looking to make the most of the exemptions that don't rely on you to survive for a certain period. The kind of things include the annual exemption, small gifts exemption, marriage exemption and the normal expenditure out of income exemption.

All of these allow you to make transfers free of IHT immediately. In summary they apply as:

Annual exemption - £3,000 per tax year, but can be carried forward for 1 year of not utilized

Small gifts exemption - £250 per gift

Marriage exemption - an exemption of up to £5,000 dependent on your relation to the people getting married

Normal expenditure out of income - no limit but it allows you to make transfers free of inheritance tax out of your income. The key to this is to show a continuing intention to make the transfer (eg by establishing the payment arrangement under a deed).

One point you will need to watch out for is how this will impact on the transferable nil rate band.

Impact on Transferable Nil Rate Band

Under the new provisions if your spouse doesn't utilise their nil rate band you'll be entitled to another nil rate band. The key to this is that your own nil rate band at the date of your death is increased by the proportion of your spouses nil rate band that wasn't utilised.

So if your spouse made a gift of £156,000 in the current tax year, prior to their death, and you died in 10 years time when the nil rate band was £500,000, you'd be entitled to your own nil rate band as well as another 50% nil rate band (ie a total of £750,000). By contrast if your spouse had not made the gift your nil rate band would have increased to £1,000,000. In this case the gift of £156,000 had caused a loss of relief for you of £250,000.

If the nil rate band was increased substantially in the future this could represent an even larger loss.

Of course this depends on the future level of the nil rate band as well as the rate at which the gifted assets increase in value.

6. REDUCE IHT WITH THE NEW 36% RATE OF INHERITANCE TAX

From 6 April 2012 people who leave at least 10% of their net estate to charity can pay a reduced rate of Inheritance Tax (IHT) of 36% instead of 40%.

This new relief is significant for anyone with an existing Will or anyone looking to make a new one. It is also significant for personal representatives administering an estate of a person who has died on or after 6 April 2012.

How does the reduced rate work?

The examples and table below show how leaving a gift to a charity in your Will can reduce your IHT liability.

James died on 12 April 2016 with an estate worth £340,000 leaving everything to his children. His available IHT threshold was £325,000 (2016/17 tax year). IHT at 40% would be payable on £15,000 (£340,000 less £325,000) so £6,000. The children receive £334,000.

Peter's position is exactly the same, except for the fact that he has left 4% of his net estate to charity in his Will.

We use "net estate" to refer to the part of his estate that would be taxable but for charity relief. (The legacy to charity could be by way of a cash legacy, a gift of specific items or a share of residue.) The children would only receive £360 less than in the example above and £600 would pass to charity.

Under the new rules, however, Peter can do much better. If instead he increases the charity legacy to 10% of his net estate, then the children still inherit the same amount, but the charity receives more and the Revenue takes the hit.

The table below shows the IHT position for James and Peter, including where Peter gives 4% or 10% of his net estate.

	James	Peter - 4% to charity	Peter -- 10% to charity
Estate on death	£340,000	£340,000	£340,000
Less IHT threshold	£325,000	£325,000	£325,000
Net estate	£15,000	£15,000	£15,000
Less charity legacy	£0	£600	£1,500
Taxable estate at 40%	£15,000	£14,400	
Taxable estate at 36%			£13,500
HMRC receive	£6,000	£5,760	£4,860
Children receive	£334,000	£333,640	£333,640
Charity receive	£0	£600	£1,500

The family members will always receive less as a result of the combined effect of the charity legacy and the tax, but the reduction in the rate of IHT should encourage charitable giving.

What happens if you do not have your full IHT threshold available?

The case studies assume that the full IHT threshold is available. If Peter had used up some or all of his IHT allowance then that would reduce the amount of the IHT threshold that could be deducted and increase the amount that would have to be given to the charity. For example, if Peter had given £150,000 to his daughter 4 years before he died then his IHT threshold would be £175,000 (£325,000 less £150,000) meaning that in order to satisfy the 10% threshold £16,500 (10% of £340,000 less £175,000) would need to be given to charity to qualify for the reduced rate.

What if you own assets jointly or are a beneficiary under a trust?

The position does get a little more complicated than the examples shown above, because as well as assets which a person owns in his own name or as tenants in common, a person's estate can also include jointly owned property and interests in certain types of trust and these will affect the tax payable. In that case the lower rate is available if 10% of your own net estate, ignoring the other components, is taxable.

You will also need to take into account exemptions and reliefs

The value of a person's estate is reduced by a number of reliefs and exemptions, such as spouse or civil partner exemption, business property relief, agricultural property relief etc. If after deducting the various reliefs and exemptions your net estate is below the IHT threshold then no IHT would be payable. It is only if, after reliefs and exemptions have been deducted the value of your net estate is over the IHT threshold, i.e. your estate is taxable, that the new rules will be advantageous to you.

Can you elect for the reduced rate not to apply?

The reduced rate of IHT will apply automatically if your estate or the component passes the 10% test. However, personal representatives can elect for the reduced rate not to apply if, for example, the benefit is likely to be minimal and the personal representatives will need to incur additional costs in valuing items left to charity to establish whether they qualify.

Do I need to change my Will?

If you have already made a Will which leaves some of your estate to charity you may wish to review this to check whether the legacy satisfies the 10% test and consider whether you want to increase the charitable legacy so that your estate can qualify for the reduced rate.

Varying a will after a death

If you are a personal representative of an estate where the deceased died on or after 6 April 2012 and did not include a charitable legacy in his Will, (eg James from the example above) or where the legacy is not sufficient to meet the 10% test (the Peter 4% to charity example), then the beneficiary/ies may wish to consider varying the Will by entering into a Deed of Variation to make or increase a charitable legacy so that the estate can benefit from the reduced rate.

7. SUMMARY OF THE TAX RELIEFS FOR CHARITABLE GIVING

Although the tax benefits of contributing to charitable causes may not be paramount for many people, it makes sense to be aware of the key reliefs available.

The main tax incentives for charitable giving are as follows:

Inheritance Tax (IHT)

- Any gifts left to charity on death under the terms of a Will are exempt from IHT
- If an individual gifts 10 per cent or more of his net estate to charity, the rate of IHT on the remaining estate (the amount over and above the available allowance currently standing at £325,000 for an individual) is reduced from 40 per cent to 36 per cent.
- Any lifetime gifts to charity pass immediately free of IHT (contrast this with a lifetime gift to an individual that must be survived by at least seven years in order for it to be seen to have left the donor's estate for IHT purposes)

Capital Gains Tax (CGT)

- Any gifts to charity of land, property or qualifying shares that have increased in value from the date of acquisition to the date of transfer will not be charged CGT on the gain (a gain on a gift to an individual on the other hand would be subject to CGT at 10/18 per cent or 20/28 per cent depending on the assets and their taxable income and gains).

Income Tax

- As long as the donor makes the appropriate Gift Aid declaration, charities are allowed to reclaim the basic rate of income tax (currently 20 per cent) on donations made to them by UK taxpayers, increasing the amount of the donation.

- Gift Aid has the following advantages for donors:

- They are able to give more without paying more
- Higher rate taxpayers can claim higher rate tax relief on their donations
- The gifts reduce taxable income so age related allowances and tax credits may increase

8. PLANNING FOR JOINT ACCOUNTS AND INHERITANCE TAX/SUCCESSION PLANNING

Many couples have joint accounts to make paying bills and arranging household finances easier.

It is not uncommon for elderly parents to ask one of their children to become a joint signatory on their bank account, to assist them in operating the account as they get older.

However, joint accounts can present several problems if one of the account holders dies. These include quantifying the extent of the deceased's share of the funds, identifying who is entitled to receive those funds and ascertaining the inheritance tax treatment.

Succession issues

Normally, the balance in a joint account will pass to the surviving account holder on death by right of survivorship, outside the terms of the deceased's Will.

This is because almost all joint accounts will be held as "joint tenants" rather than as "tenants in common".

Consequently, there is often no need to wait for probate; the survivor will simply provide the death certificate to the bank and it will transfer the money into the survivor's sole name.

The normal mandate on a joint bank account provides for this and enables either of the named parties to withdraw the whole amount for his own benefit while they are both alive. However, although this may be the starting position as regards the account holders and the bank, the parties' rights as against each other may depend on what else they have agreed and the purpose for which the account was opened and how it has been operated.

The true position may require careful consideration. This can be a difficult job of piecing together the facts and circumstances, occasionally involving acrimony, as there is usually no written evidence to clarify the position. Joint accounts are often run on the basis of an informal mutual understanding between the account holders but once one of them dies, that may be difficult to ascertain.

This was demonstrated in the case of Drakeford v Cotton and Stain, where an elderly mother set up and fully funded a joint bank account with one of her daughters.

It was agreed that when the joint account was established, the deceased had not intended to give her daughter a beneficial interest.

However, over time, the mother's intentions changed since she made it clear to the daughter and to her son that the daughter should inherit the account after her death.

The court came to this conclusion on a review of the surrounding circumstances including evidence that the mother had fallen out with her other daughter, and wished to disinherit her.

There is a long line of cases on joint bank accounts with a variety of different outcomes as each turns on its own facts. The parties' intentions are key but ideally the position should be properly documented.

Inheritance tax issues

Joint accounts are common between spouses and civil partners.

While they are both alive, interest from a joint bank account is normally taxed 50/50 as they are treated as owning the funds in equal shares. If the funds are owned in unequal shares, they will still be taxed on the 50/50 basis unless they make a joint declaration to be taxed according to their beneficial interests.

Other joint account holders will usually hold the funds as "joint tenants" and will also be taxed equally on the income unless in fact they hold the funds unequally as "tenants in common", in which case they will be subject to income tax on their share of the interest.

HMRC pays close attention to joint accounts after a death, particularly if there is a significant amount of tax at stake. They are not greatly interested in joint accounts held by spouses and civil partners where funds passing from one spouse or civil partner to the other are normally 100% exempt from inheritance tax.

However, for unmarried couples and other combinations of joint account holders, a greater degree of scrutiny will be required as to how much tax is due and who is liable for that tax.

It can not be assumed that the deceased will be treated as owning 50% of the funds and that inheritance tax will only apply to that half share.

Similarly, it can not be assumed that any inheritance tax due will be paid from the deceased's general estate; more often it will be payable by the surviving joint account holder if they inherit the funds by survivorship.

The Inheritance Tax Return that must be submitted after a death calls for a surprising amount of detail including:

- the name of the other account holder and their relationship
- to the deceased;
- the date on which the joint ownership began;
- the amount provided by each joint owner;
- how any income from the account was dealt with;
- withdrawals from the joint account.

HMRC will normally regard each account holder as beneficially entitled to the proportion of the account attributable to their contributions. So, if the deceased provided all the money, the whole amount will be subject to inheritance tax on his death.

The reservation of benefit rules are in point where a person places funds in a joint account with someone else and either receives all the interest or has the right to withdraw all the money (as is normally the case).

Withdrawals generally count against each party's contributions but where there is a lot of activity on an account, it may be extremely difficult to unravel the movements.

Any withdrawals in excess of the funds provided by each joint owner will potentially constitute a gift to the other party. This in itself has inheritance tax consequences and may also be relevant for income tax purposes.

Another case, Plum v HMRC, concerned the question of whether withdrawals from a joint bank account were taxable remittances.

An account which was funded entirely by a non domiciled UK resident was drawn on by his girlfriend in the UK. It was held that the withdrawals became the property of the girlfriend and at the time these were not taxable remittances by him.

However, since Finance Act 2008, the boyfriend would now be taxable on his girlfriend's withdrawals under the same set of circumstances as she would be a 'relevant person' in relation to him.

These recent cases serve as a reminder of some of the issues to be aware of with joint accounts, where the position may be more complicated than it first appears.

9. INHERITANCE TAX & JOINT INSURANCE POLICIES

It's reported that most holders of life insurance policies don't put their policies in trust. For most people putting the policy in trust is a common sense tax saving opportunity.

By putting it in trust it has two benefits:

- Firstly it ensures that the insurance payout is not included in your estate for inheritance tax purposes
- Secondly it ensures that your beneficiaries can access the cash quickly as it will be paid directly to them rather than having to be classed as part of the estate and subject to probate etc

There were a number of changes to the tax treatment of trusts as from 2006.

However the reason why people usually choose to have their life insurance policy written in trust is because the money can go directly to where it's needed, for example to the mortgage provider to pay off the remortgage, or to family members so they can use the tax-free money immediately.

The 2006 legislation won't affect these scenarios, because they come to an end with the death of the policyholder. It is only interest in possession trusts that would be affected by the 2006 tax changes.

The procedure for putting the policy in trust is usually very straightforward and most insurance companies will offer this for free. The documentation from the insurance policy usually includes a box to tick if you want to put it into trust. You'd then need to provide the name(s) of the beneficiary under the policy (ie who you want to benefit).

Joint life insurance policies

Certainly for individual insurance policies its pretty straightforward.

What's the position with a joint insurance policy though?

In this case the policy pays out on the death of (usually) the first to die.

Using a joint life insurance policy makes the position potentially complex and the tax treatment would depend on the specific wording of the policy. Ignoring the trust issue if you and your partner are joint policy holders there are three possibilities:

Firstly you are both beneficial tenants in common and the interest of the first to die passes under his/her will.

In this case the share of the first to die forms part of their estate and, subject to exemptions, Inheritance Tax is payable on the value of that share. Secondly you are both beneficial joint tenants and the interest of the first to die passes to the survivor.

In this case the same consequences will follow and the receipt would be potentially subject to inheritance tax.

Note that in either of these cases if you were married the spouse exemption would be available to avoid IHT on the death of the first spouse.

Finally the policy could have created unseverable contractual arrangements.(ie each policyholder holds a separate and distinct item of property).

In this case the interest of the first to die is completely extinguished at that time and does not pass either under the will or by survivorship. There is therefore no asset to tax and no inheritance tax charge.

As each insurance policy has different wording you'd therefore need to look at the policy wording to ascertain the potential tax treatment.

What about putting a joint policy in trust?

You could put a joint policy into trust. As we've seen the benefit of a trust is that it could avoid IHT on the death of the first partner.

However, writing a joint policy in trust is likely to be more complex than a single policy.

There are standard forms available from the insurance company that can allow the trust to be set up. It is usually a very straightforward process.

In many cases single life policies are preferred to a joint life policy.

The costs involved are not significantly more, but it is simpler to write into a trust and offers added protection & flexibility.

10. PUTTING LIFE INSURANCE INTO A FLEXIBLE GIFT TRUST OR BARE TRUST TO REDUCE INHERITANCE TAX

When planning for inheritance tax, any payouts under a life insurance policy can be included in your estate for inheritance tax purposes unless you arrange for the policy to be held in trust.

Putting a life insurance policy into trust is a pretty common tax planning strategy. The idea in essence is that you name the beneficiaries and the payout is then paid directly to these individuals.

It then bypasses your estate and is received directly by them. The benefit of this is that is avoids an inheritance tax charge (as it's not classed as part of your estate) and that it frees the cash up quickly as its not subject to probate.

The question is how will the transfer into a trust be treated for tax purposes?

There have been a number of changes to the tax treatment of trusts over the last few years which could impact on the treatment of the insurance policy.

Bare trust

The simplest trust option is a bare trust. For tax purposes this is not actually treated as a trust at all, and the 'beneficiary' is treated as the full beneficial owner.

So in this case if you held a life insurance policy under a bare trust you would be just the legal owner. You may pay the premiums but you wouldn't be subject to inheritance tax as it would be treated as belonging to the beneficiaries.

Most trusts for insurance policies aren't structured as bare trusts though. The insurance company will usually set up a trust structure for free when you establish a policy. If you opt for this it will usually be a flexible gift trust.

Flexible gift trust

A flexible gift trust is essentially a discretionary trust. So the trust assets (the policy) are held completely separate from both you and the beneficiaries.

The transfer into the trust would be a 'chargeable lifetime transfer' for inheritance tax purposes. As such you'd need to assess whether there would be a lifetime charge to inheritance tax when you set the trust up and transfer the policy in.

The lifetime IHT rate is 20% of the value gifted.

Firstly though if you were to die within 7 years of placing the policy into a trust (assuming the transfer is not exempt) inheritance tax may be due on the transfer depending on the value of the policy.

What is the value of the policy?

The value of the policy will usually be based on the premiums already paid or the value of the policy if it has been cashed in at that time (whichever is the highest). If this value exceeds the current nil rate band (£325,000 for 2016/2017) then inheritance tax is payable on the excess at 40%. Bear in mind that the nil rate band available is reduced by any chargeable gifts made in the previous 7 years -- ie other gifts).

If you transferred assets into a trust during your lifetime which exceeded the nil rate band then there could be a charge to the 20% lifetime IHT charge.

For most people though there won't therefore be an Inheritance tax charge on the transfer of a policy into a flexible gift trust because the value transferred is only the premiums paid into the policy which will usually be exempt (see below) or covered by the IHT nil rate band.

What about the payment of the premiums?

The payment of the premiums is treated as a gift for inheritance tax purposes. These may be exempt from IHT if they are either:

- Covered by the 'normal expenditure out of income rules'.

We've looked at these in a separate chapter but essentially you would need to show that the premiums paid were out of your income and do not reduce your standard of living.

- Covered by the IHT annual exemption (currently £3,000 pa).
-

If neither of these apply then you would need to assess whether they could be covered by the nil rate band.

Other tax charges

There are two other tax charges that should be borne in mind:

- Firstly there is the ten yearly IHT charge that applies to all discretionary trusts.

Essentially the trust itself is subject to a separate IHT regime as the trust assets are excluded from the settlors and beneficiaries estates.

The trust is subject to an IHT charge at up to 6% every 10 years.

However in practice it is unlikely that the trust would be subject to this charge. This would usually only occur if the policy had a market value over the nil rate band.

- Exit charge.

There is also a potential tax charge on the payment of proceeds to the beneficiaries. However as this is linked the 10 yearly charge as above there will only be an exit charge after 10 years if there was a 10 yearly charge as calculated above. This is for many unlikely.

Therefore most people using a flexible gift trust would not involve an IHT charge on the trust or beneficiaries. The use of a trust could therefore be very effective in avoiding inheritance tax on the eventual payout.

Note though that this assumes you aren't classed as a beneficiary of the trust. If you were this would be subject to the gift with reservation of benefit provisions and the policy payout would be classed as part of your estate. As such you should certainly ensure you aren't an actual or potential beneficiary of the trust.

11. DANGERS OF A NON BINDING SIDE LETTER FOR IHT PURPOSES

People often like to make gifts of their personal items for sentimental, rather than value, reasons. However, unexpected tax consequences can arise -- particularly where the item's true value is not appreciated at the date of the gift.

An example of this was the tale of the Bishop of Grimsby and the Chinese vase reported in the national press. The vase was owned by Mrs Rodger, had been passed down several generations of her family and Mrs Rodger has assured her niece, Jennifer Watson, that she would inherit it.

However, instead of including a specific legacy of the vase in favour of Jennifer Watson, Mrs Rodger's will contained a flexible gift of chattels with a non-binding side letter requesting her executors (among whom was the Bishop of Grimsby) to pass the vase to Jennifer Watson free of inheritance tax (IHT).

When Mrs Rodger died in March 2011, the valuer acting for the estate realised the vase was far more valuable than Mrs Rodger had realised, being worth £9 million. As IHT was payable at 40 per cent on the total value of the estate (excluding her available nil rate band allowance), the gift to Jennifer Watson free of IHT would have resulted in the rest of the estate bearing an IHT burden of over £3.6 million.

The executors therefore decided to disregard the non-binding side letter written by Mrs Rodger and to sell the vase in order to meet the IHT bill, ensuring that other assets remained in the estate to distribute to the other 31 beneficiaries.

Although initially Jennifer Watson strongly objected to a sale, a settlement was later reached allowing the vase to be sold in November 2011 for £9 million.

This case raises some interesting points for those thinking of passing on chattels.

1. Gifts on death

Consideration should be given as to whether an outright legacy under the will, or a non-binding flexible gift, is most appropriate. If a specific legacy had been included in Mrs Rodger's will, Mrs Rodger could have had greater certainty that the vase would pass to her chosen beneficiary.

However, it would have been far more difficult for the executors to mitigate the tax bill. Additionally, a flexible gift can be preferable as it allows the testator to update his wishes as to the distribution of chattels simply by writing a new letter of wishes, rather than going to the expense of amending his will. Although letters of wishes are not legally binding, they are usually followed unless there is a good reason, as there was here, not to do so.

2. Gifts during the donor's lifetime

If the donor is confident that he will have no use for the personal item during his lifetime, he may wish to give the item to his chosen beneficiary while he is alive, and have the pleasure of seeing the chosen beneficiary enjoying the item.

However, there can be IHT and capital gains tax (CGT) implications to such gifts, and potential donors should always seek to ascertain the market value of the item in question before making the gift.

(a) IHT

An outright gift to another individual will (provided the donor survives seven full years from the gift) attract no IHT charge.

However, if the donor fails to survive seven full years, unless the conditions of the gift specify otherwise, the donor's nil rate band (being the value of an estate allowed to pass tax free on death) will be reduced by the value of the gift -- and the liability of any IHT charge payable will fall on the chosen beneficiary.

Particular caution should be taken where the donor intends to make a gift of a personal item but still benefit from the item gifted in some way as, even where such gifts are made more than seven years before death, they can still be caught by the "reservation of benefit" rules for IHT purposes.

An example of this would be if Mrs Rodger had given the vase to Jennifer Watson by formal deed of gift but then retained the vase on her own mantelpiece during her lifetime.

Essentially, if the donor continues to receive some benefit from the asset in question in the seven years immediately before his death, the value of the asset is taken into account for IHT purposes on his death, increasing the value of the donor's estate for IHT purposes long after the donor thought that he had dealt with this problem.

While it is possible for a donor to continue to benefit from an item gifted in certain circumstances, the exemptions available are complex and advice should always be sought on such gifts.

(b) CGT

Although no information is available on the value of the vase when Mrs Rodger inherited it (its "base cost" for CGT purposes), if we assume for the sake of argument that it was worth £2 million on acquisition, then, to put it simply, a gift to an individual during her lifetime would have triggered a "deemed gain" of £7 million, charged to CGT at 28 percent ie, a £1.96 million CGT bill (note that if the disposal was after 5 April 2016 the rate would be 20 percent).

In some cases, where an asset has built up significant value during its period of ownership, it may be worth considering keeping it in the potential donor's estate until death, as there will be an uplift in the base cost for CGT purposes on death.

For example, if Jennifer Watson had received the vase from Mrs Rodger's estate, her base cost for CGT purposes would have been £9 million and, if she had subsequently disposed of the vase for £10 million, there would only have been CGT to pay on the £1 million gain in the value of the vase since Mrs Rodger's death.

Keeping an asset in an individual's estate could, of course, have unpleasant IHT implications. However, if IHT charges can be avoided on the owner's death, for example, by providing for the asset to pass to the individual's surviving spouse (securing the spouse exemption), the spouse can then give the asset to the chosen beneficiary shortly afterwards, with little or no CGT to pay.

The spouse needs to live at least seven years from the date of their gift to avoid the asset being taken into account as part of his or her own estate for IHT purposes. It may be appropriate for the spouse to take out term insurance against this risk.

Making a gift of a personal item to a person can be straightforward, depending on the gift and its value.

However, complications can arise, and it is prudent:

1. to make sure that the donor has an up-to-date market value of any such personal items he may wish to give to another person, either during his lifetime or by will; and

2. to obtain proper advice on the tax implications of gifts of such personal items.

It is particularly important to obtain proper advice where the donor wishes to retain any use or enjoyment of the asset gifted after the gift is made, as such a reservation of benefit may render all the inheritance tax planning in relation to such a gift pointless.

12. INHERITANCE TAX PLANNING FOR THE FAMILY HOME

For many people, their home is their most valuable asset and can give rise to a significant IHT liability on their death (or the death of the surviving spouse). The classic issue for many people is that, on the one hand, they would like to mitigate the IHT liability, but at the same time they would like to remain living in their home.

How can an individual give away their main residence in order to mitigate their future inheritance tax (IHT) liability and continue to occupy, without being caught by the reservation of benefit provisions?

What do the current IHT rules say?

The IHT legislation includes a set of rules known as the "Gifts with Reservation of Benefit Rules".

These complex rules mean that even though you have given an asset away, if you continue to derive a benefit from it (e.g. you give away your home but you continue to live there) you are treated as if you still own it - and it therefore forms part of your taxable estate on death.

Over the years there have been a number of ways of circumventing this problem. The approach that is currently most readily accepted by HMRC is to pay a market rent for your occupation under a secure lease.

Transferring your home to a trust or your children

Typically, this involves two valuers being instructed: one for the homeowner(s) as future tenant(s); and the other for the future owner of the freehold, as landlord(s).

Sometimes this will be the owners' children, but often this is the home owners as trustees of a new family trust, which gives additional security as they retain control of the freehold through this role. The valuers will agree the current market rent between them.

A secure lease is then granted to the homeowner(s), at a market rent and for an appropriate term. The freehold of the property is then transferred to a trust or to their children, subject to the lease.

If the homeowner(s) survive the transfer by seven years and continues to pay the full rent, the value of the freehold (or a share of it) will be entirely outside their estate for IHT purposes. If the homeowner(s) are not confident they can afford the full rent for the property, they can transfer a percentage interest in the house, rather than the whole.

The advantages to using a trust structure

There are a number of advantages to using the trust structure.

- The homeowner(s) can be trustees of the trust, which enables them to retain a degree of control and ensures their interests cannot be overridden without their consent. The terms of the lease will also be drafted to help protect their interests. The rental payments also decrease the value in the homeowner's taxable estate immediately.
- The rental payments received by the trustees can be used to benefit future generations either immediately or by income being accumulated to capital. It also provides the flexibility to divert income to beneficiaries with lower income tax rates (eg, grandchildren) to ensure maximum income tax efficiency.
- Using a trust structure ensures both the property and the income arising can be protected from divorce or bankruptcy of beneficiaries.

With proper advice, homeowner(s) can gift all (or a share) of their home to their family to save a significant amount of IHT and retain a secure right of occupation. The caveats to this are that the homeowner(s) need to survive the gift by seven years and can afford to pay the rent.

There are a number of more involved approaches to saving IHT, but the rental approach is the most "tried and tested" and in many ways the simplest.

13. REDUCING CGT, IHT AND INCOME TAX ON A PROPERTY INVESTMENT PORTFOLIO BY USING MORTGAGES

Although the property prices have reduced significantly in the last few years many buy to let ('BTL') landlords will still be faced with a large potential inheritance tax charge.

With IHT at 40% on amounts in excess of the nil rate band (£325,000 for 16/17) it's easy to see how a substantial IHT liability could arise.

Gifting an interest in the property

The easiest way to avoid IHT is to simply transfer an interest in property to your children or other family members.

This would be a Potentially Exempt Transfer ('PET') and provided you survived at least 7 years from the date of transfer the value transferred would be excluded from your estate for inheritance tax purposes. You would not need to do anything specific for it to qualify as a PET. Provided the beneficial interest in the property/share of the property was transferred to your children/family it would be a PET.

Note that this assumes you do not retain any interest in the part of the property that is transferred. If you for example transferred a share in the property then continued to occupy it or if you received the rental income this would be classed as a gift with reservation of benefit ('GROB') and as such the value transferred to your children/family would remain within your estate (unless you paid a market rental for your occupation, as in the last chapter).

So a direct gift can clearly be effective in taking the BTL properties out of your estate after 7 years, however the two main drawbacks with a transfer of the properties to your children/family are:

Firstly - The transfer to your children is a disposal for capital gains tax ('CGT') purposes. As you are classed as connected parties the disposal consideration is deemed to be the market value of the properties. You would therefore crystallise a capital gain based on the uplift in market value since the date you acquired it.

If they have been your main residence at any point you could qualify for PPR relief to further reduce the gain. The remaining gain after the annual exemptions (worth around £22,000 for the two of you) would then be charged at 18% or 28% (depending your other income/gains).

If the properties have reduced in value in the current market the gain may not be significant depending on when you did purchase.

Secondly - The other problem is that your children/family would hold the properties at the current market value. On a future disposal by them they would be subject to CGT (assuming they're not occupied as their main residence).

On the assumption that property prices will begin to rise again, they could be taxed on a significant uplift in value on a future disposal. By contrast if the properties are left to them via the will they would hold at the probate value (ie the market value at death).

This would then substantially reduce the CGT charge on a future disposal. The downside of course would be IHT.

The other ancillary problem is that once you've transferred the property, in order to avoid the gift with reservation of benefit provisions you would not be able to obtain a benefit from the rental income. This would therefore be received by (and taxed on) your children/family who now own the property.

Releasing cash as debt

Another option could be to raise debt on the property and gift this to the children rather than actually gifting the property. This could have a number of advantages:

1) This would be a PET and exempt after 7 years as above. The debt would however still reduce the value for IHT purposes. Therefore the net effect of this would be similar to a transfer of the actual property and there could be an IHT exemption after 7 years.

2) There would be no CGT charge on the transfer of cash to your children/family as cash is not a chargeable asset. This would therefore be much more attractive than a transfer of the actual property as you'd be able to avoid any tax charge on transfer.

3) You would continue to own the property. You could then leave it to your children/family in your will so that they would inherit at the then market value. The debt secured against the property would reduce it's value for IHT purposes. This would therefore reduce the future capital gain on a disposal by your children/family members.

4) As you're the legal owner of the property you would retain the rental income in your name.
However the interest on the debt may be able to be claimed as an income tax deduction when calculating the rental profits. This is on the basis that the debt is a withdrawal of capital from the rental business (and there is no overdrawn capital account).

By raising debt against a BTL property and gifting this you could therefore see a number of tax advantages. Not only will any CGT charge be avoided but you could still get the IHT benefits and there could also be an income tax benefit.

14. SAVE INHERITANCE TAX ON YOUR INVESTMENT PROPERTIES

With rates of inheritance tax at 40%, this can represent a huge chunk of your wealth that goes to the taxman. Anyone with a substantial estate will therefore be looking at opportunities to reduce the potential Inheritance tax charge in the future.

Even with the slow property market, property investors could be looking at huge inheritance tax liabilities. OK, the amount of any mortgage is deducted before Inheritance tax is charged, but nevertheless the net estate could be huge.

One of the problems for anyone with investment property who is also looking to reduce inheritance tax is that simply gifting the properties to children or grandchildren will in many cases not be tax efficient. Although from an inheritance perspective it will be excluded from their estate after 7 years, the transfer would also be a disposal for capital gains tax purposes.

For capital gains tax, any mortgages are excluded and the gain will essentially represent the uplift in value. Of course the capital gains tax rate is 28% for higher rate taxpayers on disposal of UK residential property so the tax charge could be substantial.

One option to 'have your cake and eat it' is to use a property investment trust.

The trust could be established as a discretionary trust or even an interest in possession trust. In both cases they would still be 'relevant property trusts'.

Relevant property trusts are treated as a separate entity to the settlor (ie the person who makes the transfer), and therefore property held within such a trust will usually be excluded from the settlors estate for inheritance tax purposes. The two provisos here are:

- they still need to survive for at least seven years from the date of the transfer.

- the settlor and his wife need to ensure that they don't retain the right to benefit from the trust. If they do, anti avoidance rules (known as the reservation of benefit provisions) can apply to treat the property transferred as part of the settlors estate

What about capital gains tax?

The transfer to the trust is still a disposal for capital gains tax purposes, however it's possible to holdover the capital gain on the transfer. The trustees can also holdover the gain if they transfer the property to a trust beneficiary in the future. Effectively this means that the eventual beneficiary will hold the property at the same cost that the settlor had.

To claim holdover relief though it's important that the settlor their spouse and any minor children can't benefit from the trust. You'll therefore need to make the trust for the benefit of:

- Uncles
- Adult children
- Grandchildren
- Brothers
- Sisters
- Aunts
- Nephews
- Nieces
- Cousins
- Separated couples
- Divorced couples
- Relatives of your partner you are living with (if you're not married or in a civil partnership with your partner)
- Relatives of divorced parties

It's also worth noting that you can't use this and also claim principal private residence ('PPR') relief. So, you couldn't transfer a property to a trust for the benefit of your adult children, claim holdover relief to defer the gain and also have the trustees claiming PPR relief on the basis it was his main residence.

Downsides

This all sounds pretty good. Transfer investment property to a trust for adult children or grandchildren. Defer any gain and avoid IHT after 7 years.

It is good…but the downside is that the trust itself is subject to a separate inheritance tax regime. This can get very complicated however essentially there are 3 key points when inheritance tax can be an issue:

- On the transfer to the trust
- After 10 years
- On the transfer of properties out of the trust

Nevertheless there is good way to minimise the effect of the provisions. This relies on using the inheritance tax nil rate band.

This is currently fixed at £325,000. Assuming no other transfers in the previous 7 years you could transfer a property to the trust with a value of up to this amount free of any inheritance tax to the trust.

If, as many people do, properties are owned jointly this means you could transfer a value of up to £650,000 to the trust. In fact when you take into account the annual inheritance tax exemption it will be slightly more than this. Each person has a £3,000 annual exemption that is deducted from gifts before inheritance tax is taken into account. As a bonus this can be carried forward for 1 year.

This means that as a couple you could transfer a property with a value of up to £662,000 into the trust tax free. This could easily represent a couple of properties and represents a CGT free transfer.

It would also be free of inheritance tax after seven years.

This could then be repeated seven years later to take account of the new 'untouched' inheritance tax threshold. Assuming this was £400,000, you could transfer £812,000 as a couple.

Over the course of 20 years or so this would easily allow £2,000,000 worth of properties to be transferred out of the estate. This would save inheritance tax of £800,000 and also be free from capital gains tax.

This £800,000 inheritance tax saving is not though a complete picture. The trust would also need to consider it's own position. It will be subject to an inheritance tax charge on the value of the trust assets every 10 years.

The extent of any inheritance tax charge would depend on the value of the trust asset as well as the nil rate band at that point.

If we assume that a couple transferred property worth £662,000 into a trust, and then 7 years later transferred property worth a further £812,000 into the trust the cost of the trust assets would be £1.474M. Assuming that these properties have now grown to £2,000,000.

The nil rate band may be £500,000.

The 10 year tax charge in the trust is calculated as:

Trust Assets	£2,000,000
Nil rate bands	-£1,000,000
Chargeable amount in the trust	£1,000,000
IHT charge at 20%	£200,000
Effective rate	£200,000/£2,000,000*3/10 = 3%

There is then a reduction in this for each calendar quarter that the properties were in the trust.

Therefore the property in the trust originally would be taxed at 3% and the property transferred in after 7 years would be charged at 2.1%. The inheritance tax charge could therefore be in the region of £50,000.

Although not an insignificant amount, when compared to the value of the assets in the trust (£2,000,000) and the potential IHT charge if held personally (£800,000) it represents a considerable inheritance tax saving.

15. INHERITANCE TAX AND YOUR FAMILY COMPANY

Given the current rate of Inheritance tax is 40% this can represent a substantial tax charge, particularly if you have valuable assets such as shares in your family company.

The key relief for inheritance tax is business property relief ('BPR'). This provides for a 100% relief against the value of shares in an unquoted trading company. Therefore if your shareholding qualified it would effectively be excluded from your estate for IHT purposes.

Ensuring that your shareholding qualifies for full BPR can reap dividends as this would then avoid the 40% tax charge on the value of the shareholding.

However, as you'd expect this is not straightforward and there are a number of obstacles to gaining full relief.

Obstacles to full BPR relief

Firstly BPR is not due where the business carried on by the company, consists wholly or mainly of making or holding of investments.

There is no statutory definition of 'wholly or mainly' and HMRC would look at the main activities of the business, and to its assets and sources of income or gains, over a reasonable period. If your company was wholly or mainly involved in the holding of investments no BPR would be due.

Assessing whether the company is involved 'wholly or mainly' in investment activities can be complex. HMRC would look at the accounts and assess the assets, income and time involved in the relevant activities to assess whether the investment aspect exceeded 50% of the total activities.

Any type of investment activities can be taken into account for this, however the most common are having substantial cash balances and also let properties on the balance sheet.

A review of the accounts by HMRC would instantly highlight these assets and they would then look in detail at whether the company was 'wholly or mainly involved in an investment activity. In many cases the investment activities of the company would not make the company an investment company. However there can still be a restriction.

Note that if the company fails the test above and is wholly or mainly involved in an investment activity there would be no BPR.

Property held outside the company

Most businesses start life as qualifying trading businesses or companies for IHT. And in the early days of an entrepreneur's career, avoiding IHT is unlikely to be on their radar. The problems come later as the business grows and acquires value.

The business owner may, for example, decide to incorporate to reduce their income tax liabilities. And the accountant may quite sensibly advise for the business premises to be retained outside the limited company.

If you own 100% of the business premises and more than half the company shares, you will get 50% business property relief on the business premises. So you only avoid IHT on half the value. If you control less than half of the company and you own the business premises personally, you may not get business property relief at all.

Excepted assets

The other restriction applies a proportionate restriction for any 'excepted assets'. Excepted assets are assets that are not:

- used mainly for business purposes in the last two years (or, if shorter, their period of ownership).
- required for future use in the business at the time of the transfer/death.

It's important to note that cash balances can be excepted assets, to the extent that they are not required for day to day activities or for specific business plans.

Therefore if you had substantial levels of cash in your company you would need to be able to support the use of the cash in the company.

For instance are you looking at a potential acquisition or the purchase of new machinery etc. Is the cash required for other business purposes eg a buffer in the case of legal claims etc. If there is a viable business reason for the holding of the cash this could ensure that the cash was not an excepted asset.

It should also be noted that 'business purposes' is much broader than 'trading activities'.

Therefore if the company includes both a trading activity and property investment, providing the extent of the property investment business does not cause the shares to fail the first test (above), it could be argued that the property investment assets are not excepted assets, as they are used for business purposes.

HMRC have been known to challenge this on the basis that the investment activity is not a business (usually due to lack of active involvement by the directors).

If some of the assets of the company are excepted assets the amount of the transfer qualifying for BPR, is the value of the shares gifted multiplied by the fraction below:

Gift x Total assets - Excepted assets/Total assets

There would then be a proportionate restriction in the amount of BPR.

If there is a risk that there could be a restriction in BPR consideration should be given to extracting the cash from the company tax efficiently.

BPR and Loans

In the 2013 Budget, the Chancellor made some changes to restrict the availability of business property relief (BPR) where borrowing is used to fund the BPR qualifying investments.

This means that business property relief will be restricted if the relevant BPR asset was acquired using debt.

Example

Jack, who is single and has already used his nil rate IHT band, has assets worth a total of £1 million and borrowings of £250,000.

Included within Jacks assets are his company shares, now worth £500,000. He bought these shares for £250,000, having raised the funds by borrowing against his £500,000 home. His unquoted company meets the BPR criteria of being a mainly or wholly trading company, which doesn't own any investment assets, and he has owned his shares for over two years. On this basis he will qualify for 100% business property relief.

Until the 2013 legislation, essentially the debt in this example would be set against the chargeable assets other than the shares (ie the house) for IHT calculation purposes leaving the value of his shares covered wholly by the BPR available. His IHT liability is therefore £250,000 x 40% = £100,000. This is made up of £1 million of assets, less £250,000 debt, less £500,000 BPR.

Following the introduction of the new restrictions, Jack's potential IHT liability will be £500,000 x 40% = £200,000 -- double the amount. This is because the debt is set against the asset it was actually used to purchase -- in this case the shares. So whereas previously the BPR was worth £500,000 to Jack, he will in future only receive BPR of £250,000 leaving the house subject to IHT in full.

Even if the arrangements were made before the new rules will be introduced, Jack will have an increased potential IHT liability of £100,000.

Borrowing purpose is key

Had Jack had a mortgage secured against his home and used other cash to acquire the shares, he would be unaffected by the change in rules -- the key is the purpose of the borrowing and being able to clearly demonstrate that purpose.

16. AIM SHARES & IHT RELIEF

Following on from the last chapter, we're often asked about shares listed on the "Alternative Investment Market" and how they are are treated for IHT purposes.

As we've seen 'Business Property Relief' provides for tax relief to the extent that assets consist of 'relevant business property'. The rates of relief for different types of 'relevant business property' include:

- property consisting of a business or interest in a business = 100%
- control holdings of unquoted securities = 100%
- unquoted shares = 100%
- control holdings of quoted shares = 50%

These rates of relief apply to both assets gifted as well as assets held at the date of death.

What does unquoted mean?

Unquoted means not quoted on a recognised stock exchange. Shares dealt in on the Alternative Investment Market ('AIM') are unquoted. Shares quoted on the NASDAQ are however quoted.

This means that in terms of AIM shares you don't need to have a control holding to qualify for BPR relief.

Do all AIM shares qualify?

No they don't. BPR is specifically excluded where a business carried on by a company, consists wholly or mainly of:

- dealing in securities, stocks and shares;
- dealing in land or buildings, or
- making or holding of investments

So any investment companies won't qualify for relief and neither would any property developers. However, building/construction firms could still qualify.

Ownership requirement

In all cases there is a general requirement that in order to qualify for BPR the shares would need to have been owned by you throughout the two years immediately before the transfer. So unless you'd owned them for two years at the date of your death or date of gift there would be no BPR relief.

Exceptions

There are though some exceptions to the two year ownership requirement. You can still qualify for BPR relief even if you haven't owned for two years:

- where you became entitled to the property on the death of another person, and they had qualified
- where the property transferred replaced other qualifying property, and
- where the property transferred had been acquired on an earlier transfer within the two year period.

Lifetime transfers

The above represents the rules that apply to assets (including AIM shares) that you hold on your death. What about AIM shares that you gift during your lifetime and which are still caught within the inheritance tax net?

Well there are additional conditions to determine whether business relief is due on lifetime transfers. These conditions are broadly designed to deny relief if the transferee has disposed of the business property without replacement or if it is no longer 'relevant business property' (eg the company becomes an investment company).

What conditions need to be satisfied for gifted shares?

Two conditions have to be satisfied for business property relief to be available. These are:

- the original shares must have been owned by the transferee (ie the person who the shares were gifted to) throughout the period between the date of the transfer and the death of the transferor (or earlier death of the transferee),
- the shares must still be 'relevant business property' immediately before the death of the transferor (or earlier death of the transferee).

These means that for all intents and purposes AIM shares will qualify for 100% inheritance tax relief provided:

- the company is a trading company
- you have owned the shares for at least 2 years
- if you gift the shares they are still owned by the person you gift them to at the date of your death (and the shares still qualify) or they have reinvested into other qualifying property

17. QUALIFYING FOR INHERITANCE TAX RELIEF ON COMPANIES WITH LARGE CASH BALANCES

Any shares that you own would be included in your estate and potentially subject to 40% Inheritance Tax (IHT).

However, as we've seen if the company is an unquoted trading company you should consider whether business property relief would apply. This can provide for a 100% exemption from inheritance tax.

Where an unquoted trading company holds an amount of cash which is in excess of the amount which is needs for its business, it is likely that the cash will be treated as an excepted asset and excluded from business property relief.

This is because under IHTA84/S112 (1) the value of any "excepted assets" is to be left out of account for the purposes of business relief. In order not to be "excepted" an asset must pass one of two tests:

• It must have been used wholly or mainly for the purposes of the business in question throughout the two years, immediately preceding the gift or date of death

• Alternatively it must be required at the time of the transfer of value for future use for the purposes of the business in question.

If the cash is surplus to requirements then it could be viewed as an excepted asset with the result that the amount of Business Property Relief ("BPR") on the shares would be restricted.

If however there was a sound commercial reason for the build up of cash you could argue that it did not constitute an excepted asset.

It has been pointed out to HMRC recently that in the current economic climate many businesses are retaining increased cash reserves to protect themselves against any further downtown in trade.

However, HMRC are not impressed. They say that to avoid treatment as an excepted asset there needs to be evidence that the cash is held for an identifiable future purpose.

This may in fact be overstating the position. Section 112 only requires the cash to be required for the future use for the purposes of the business. There may therefore be a number of things in contemplation.

HMRC consider that the holding of funds as a buffer to weather the economic climate is not sufficient reason to prevent it being an excepted asset.

What to do?

HMRC may be viewing the position unsympathetically but the taxpayer is able to protect himself here.

The problem is that the holding of cash on deposit is not generally regarded as an investment business by reason of the decision in Barclays Bank Trust Co v CIR.

It therefore represents an excepted asset if it is not required for the future use in the business.

However, if this surplus cash were to be invested otherwise than on pure cash deposit, then it would become an investment business and providing this investment business was not more important than the overall trading business, then it would not be an excepted asset and no problem would arise.

The company would still be wholly or mainly a trading company and the existence of the subservient investment business would not interfere with the business property relief.

18. THE TRANSFERABLE NIL RATE BAND

The transferable nil rate band is a massive tax break for most married couples (or civil partners). It effectively ensures that on the death of a surviving spouse they and their deceased spouse have had the benefit of two nil rate bands against their estate.

So a couple with a house of £600,000 and £50,000 in the bank will be able to pass on their assets to their children free of inheritance tax due to the combined nil rate bands.

In actual fact its more beneficial than this as it applies by looking at the nil rate band in existence when the first spouse died and working out what proportion of this was not used. The current nil rate band is uplifted by this amount. So you can get another nil rate band not at the rate on the death of the first spouse but at the current rate.

The calculation is pretty simple.

- You take the nil rate band at the date of the first spouses
- death ('A')
- You work out what amount of this they have left ('B')
- You divide A by B (A/B)
- You then multiply this by the current nil rate band

So the most you can get is another nil rate band equivalent to the current one.

When working out what share of the nil rate band is left after the first spouses death you essentially need to take out anything that was a chargeable transfer. This will therefore be transfers to anyone other than the spouse which isn't covered by an inheritance tax relief (such as business property relief).

Examples

1. Jack died with no assets. His wife held all the assets in her name.

His wife died a number of years later and would be entitled to offset two nil rate bands on her death. Jack still had his full nil rate band available from his death.

2. Mary died with an estate of £500,000. She left all of this to her husband. The husband then died many years later. Again her could offset two nil rate bands as Mary's full nil rate band was available for offset.

Supporting documents

You should ensure that you can get hold of the following (if applicable):

- The first spouses death certificate
- Their marriage certificate
- A copy of their will
- A copy of the grant of probate
- A copy of any deed of variation that changed who inherited the assets of the estate.

You're looking for evidence to show that they were married at the date of the first spouses death and to show what happened to their estate (ie what it consisted of and who it was left to)

19. USING A PARALLEL COMPANY TO REDUCE INHERITANCE TAX

Shareholders in small companies will no doubt consider their inheritance tax position. In most cases of course business property relief ('BPR') will eliminate any inheritance tax charge. This will apply to shares in unquoted trading companies.

There are however a number of caveats to this relief, most notably:

- the company's business must not consist wholly or mainly of dealing in securities, stocks or shares or land or buildings
- the business must not consist wholly or mainly of making or holding investments (unless the company is a holding company).
- at the time of transfer the company must not be in liquidation
- the shares must be owned for at least 2 years before the transfer
- there mustn't be a contract for the sale of the shares at the date of the gift
- relief is restricted if the company has some investment assets

There are therefore a number of ways that BPR could be restricted or event eliminated in full. Common instances are property traders, where there's large investment assets on the balance sheet and where shares have been owned for a short period.

If BPR isn't due at all this raises the prospect of a 40% inheritance tax charge on the value of the shares. What can be done if BPR isn't due?

Well the first issue should be to transfer the shares as soon as possible. CGT would also need to be considered, however, in terms of inheritance tax if they survive for 7 years the value of the shares would be excluded from their estate for tax purposes.

Even if they survive for at least 3 years this will reduce the tax on the gift itself by up to 80%, even though it doesn't effect the rate on the rest of the estate.

The transfer would be a disposal for capital gains tax purposes. As such the proceeds would be likely to be the market value, and the gain could be substantial.

On the plus side there's Entrepreneurs Relief that could reduce the rate of tax to 10%.

There's also gift relief that will frequently be available to defer any gain until the recipient sells the shares (or emigrates within 6 years).

Aside from gifting what else could be considered?

There are a couple of other options that could be considered, however one of the most popular would be to use a parallel company. This can be particularly beneficial if the shareholders in the main company don't want to transfer their shares (for whatever reason).

Using a parallel company

A parallel company is a company with different shareholders to the company company. Frequently this will be put the intended beneficiaries as the shareholders in the parallel company (eg children). The plan would be to engage in new ventures that would normally have been carried out via the main company. A more aggressive use of the parallel company would be to take on new customers.

You'd need to be careful to ensure that there is no transfer of value our of the existing company to the new parallel company. The danger in this would be:

- This would be classed as a disposal of goodwill by the existing company to the new parallel company, and
- This could give rise to an inheritance tax disposal by the shareholders in the existing disposal and it would be classed as a chargeable lifetime transfer (like a transfer to a trust).

The plan behind the use of the parallel company is that it would grow in value, whilst the existing company would retain the same value or even reduce in value. It would be outside the scope of the shareholders (in the main company) estate and free from inheritance tax on their death. For any business that is growing this could represent a significant tax saving.

How to set up the parallel company

There are a few points that should be observed if looking at establishing a separate parallel company:

- The parallel company should not be taking over existing customers and
- It also shouldn't take on any customer that specifically approaches the old company
- There should also be independent/third party finance for the parallel company

The aim with all of these is to show that there is no transfer from the existing company to the new parallel company. Instead you'd be looking to show that any reduction in value of the existing company didn't arise from any transfer but instead by the existing company being less competitive than the new parallel company (which is why it is growing in business).

The parallel company could then be an effective method for transferring value out of the estate of individual shareholders, which would be particularly beneficial if BPR would not otherwise be available.

20. REDUCING INHERITANCE TAX WITH A DOUBLE TAX TREATY

The UK has lots of double tax treaties - well over a hundred in fact.

However these treaties are income tax treaties, and although they're useful for assessing the tax position on any income or capital gains arising to you either here or overseas, they're completely useless if you're trying to assess your Inheritance tax position. The reason for this is that the 'Taxes Covered' section of the income tax treaties do not cover Inheritance tax.

In fact the UK does have some Inheritance tax treaties, however these are much fewer in number. There are about nine in total and this includes treaties with France, Switzerland, Italy, India, South Africa, the US and Sweden. The technical name for these are 'Estate and Inheritance tax agreements' and they essentially apply to determine how each country will share out the Inheritance tax take between themselves.

Importance of domicile

The key issue in terms of UK Inheritance tax is domicile. Forget residence and even ordinary residence, Inheritance tax looks at something much more substantive. I won't go into to the rules surrounding domicile here, as we look at this in a later chapter but suffice it to say that you will be a foreign domiciliary if your father was, and you will only lose a UK domicile if you can show that you leave the UK in what will be a permanent departure.

As well as domicile, the location of assets is also important. For UK tax purposes, the UK Revenue will tax:

- A UK domiciliary on their worldwide estate,
- A non UK domiciliary on their UK estate only

An estate tax treaty will be relevant where someone is liable to Inheritance tax in more than one country. This could be a UK domiciliary with assets overseas. In this case the overseas assets would be within the scope of UK taxes, and also within the scope of overseas tax as many countries also adopt the UK rules and tax assets within their jurisdiction.

There is also a much wider interpretation which arises because a person can remain UK domiciled even if they don't set foot in the UK for ten years.

As many overseas countries base inheritance tax on residence, you could see two countries looking to tax all of a deceased's worldwide assets. The UK on the basis of a UK domicile and the overseas country on the basis of residence.

The treaty will be very important in these cases as it allows the allocation of taxing rights between the two countries.

Why establishing treaty domicile in another state is important

The UK estate tax treaties specifically provide for the UK domicile rules to apply, but they then also address the case where two countries are claiming worldwide taxing rights. Lets have a look at an extract from a treaty and see exactly what it states. In this case we'll look at the UK-Switzerland treaty:

Article 4
Fiscal domicile

(1) For the purposes of this Convention, a deceased person was domiciled:
(a) in the United Kingdom if he was domiciled in the United Kingdom in accordance with the law of the United Kingdom or is treated as so domiciled for the purposes of a tax which is the subject of the Convention; (b) in Switzerland if he was domiciled or was resident in Switzerland in accordance with the law of Switzerland or if he was a Swiss national and Swiss civil law requires his succession to be ruled in Switzerland.

Note that the Convention defines the scope of fiscal domicile separately for the UK and for Switzerland. In the case of the UK it will also include the deemed domicile rules. These state that a person will be deemed to be UK domiciled for inheritance tax purposes if they are resident in the UK for 17 out of the previous 20 years and also for three years after they actually lose UK domicile status. As of April 2017, individuals will be deemed to be UK domiciled if they have been UK resident in least fifteen of the twenty tax years immediately preceding the tax year in question.

However, a deceased person shall be deemed not to be domiciled in one of the States if that State imposes tax only by reference to property situated in that State.

So, a UK domiciliary owning property in Switzerland would not be classed as Swiss domiciled just by reason of owning property there.

(2) Where by reason of the provisions of paragraph (1) of this Article a deceased person was domiciled in both States, then, subject to the provisions of the attached Protocol, his status shall be determined as follows:

(a) he shall be deemed to have been domiciled in the State in which he had a permanent home available to him; if he had a permanent home available to him in both States, he shall be deemed to have been domiciled in the State with which his personal and economic relations were closer (centre of vital interests);
(b) if the State in which he had his centre of vital interests cannot be determined, or if he did not have a permanent home available to him in either State, he shall be deemed to have been domiciled in the
State in which he had an habitual abode;
(c) if he had an habitual abode in both States or in neither of them, he shall be deemed to have been domiciled in the State of which he was a national;
(d) if he was a national of both States or of neither of them, the competent authorities of the Contracting States shall settle the question by mutual agreement.

This is how the treaty determines which country will have primary taxing rights for Inheritance tax purposes. These are exactly the same tests as many income tax treaties apply, in that it will be necessary to first look at the country of permanent residence, and if this does not determine domicile, the centre of vital interests would be determined.

It is rarely necessary to look at other issues, but if necessary habitual abode and nationality could also be looked at.

Therefore if a UK domiciliary had property in the UK and Switzerland, but was a resident of Switzerland, the treaty would usually apply to give Switzerland taxing rights over the worldwide estate. If this individual also had assets located overseas this could be lead to a significant tax saving given that Swiss rates of Inheritance tax are much lower than the UK rates.

In this respect obtaining permanent residence in a treaty country can be highly beneficial for UK domiciliaries as it can eliminate the potential risk of a UK Inheritance tax charge on your worldwide estate. Instead you'll just be taxed in the overseas country.

Given that the UK has estate tax treaties with:

- Ireland
- South Africa
- USA
- Netherlands
- Sweden
- Switzerland
- France
- Italy

it makes sense if you're planning to emigrate to any of these to establish treaty domicile there (eg a permanent home there) to avoid the risk of double taxation.

Real estate located overseas
Article 5
Immovable property

(1) Immovable property which forms part of the estate of a person domiciled in a Contracting State and which is situated in the other Contracting State may be taxed in that other State.

(2)

(2) The term "immovable property" shall have the meaning which it has under the law of the Contracting State in which the property in question is situated provided always that debts secured by mortgage or otherwise shall not be regarded as

immovable property. The term shall in any case include property accessory to immovable property, livestock and equipment used in agriculture and forestry, rights to which the provisions of general law respecting landed property apply, an interest in the proceeds of sale of land which is held on trust for sale, usufruct of immovable property and rights to variable or fixed payments as consideration for the working of, or the right to work, mineral deposits, sources and other natural resources; ships and aircraft shall not be regarded as immovable property.

(3) The provisions of paragraphs (1) and (2) of this Article shall also apply to immovable property of an enterprise and to immovable property used for the performance of professional services or other activities of an independent character.

This states that immovable property (ie land and property/real estate) which forms part of a deceased person's estate may be taxed in the country of domicile and in the country where the property is located.

Where property is taxable in both countries the Convention resolves potential double taxation: in two ways:

- providing for the UK to give credit for Swiss tax on immovable property and business property situated in Switzerland, and
- by providing for Switzerland to exempt UK land and property and business property

Therefore there is no exemption from tax, but a simple credit for any overseas tax suffered. This ties in with the UK rules so that even if you are a non UK domiciliary you will still be subject to UK inheritance tax on any UK source assets (which would clearly include UK property and from April 2017 UK residential property held via an offshore structure).

The five year 'extension'

Based on the above a UK domiciliary could be taxed on Swiss property in both the UK and Switzerland, whereas someone who was Swiss domiciled by virtue of the treaty would only be charged to

Swiss Inheritance taxes.

This is correct, however the treaty does make further provisions which state that the UK can tax property situated in Switzerland where the deceased person was UK domiciled at death or had been UK domiciled within the previous 5 years, and was a national of the UK and was not a Swiss national.

This is also extended to property situated in other countries if at any time within 5 years of the death the deceased had been domiciled in the UK and again was a national of the UK and was not a Swiss national.

The relevant extract states:

(3) Any property which is situated in Switzerland and which would be taxable only in Switzerland under paragraph (1)(a)(ii) of this Article may also be taxed in the United Kingdom if the deceased was:

(a) by virtue of the provisions of paragraph (2) of Article 4 domiciled in the United Kingdom at the time of his death; or
(b) by virtue of those provisions domiciled in Switzerland at the time of his death but (i) had been domiciled in the United Kingdom at any time within the five years preceding his death; and (ii) was at that time a national of the United Kingdom without being a national of Switzerland.

(4) Any property which is not situated in either Contracting State and which would be taxable only in Switzerland under paragraph (1)(b) (ii) of this Article may also be taxed in the United Kingdom if the deceased:
(a) had been domiciled in the United Kingdom at any time within the five years preceding his death; and
(b) was at that time a national of the United Kingdom without being a national of Switzerland.

This therefore effectively provides for a five year extension to the domicile rules such that even if you lose your UK domicile you can still be taxed on property in other countries if you retain your UK nationality for a period of five years after you lose your UK domicile status.

It is therefore important to lose your UK domicile status, sooner rather than later and keep records of the various indicators (eg closing UK bank accounts, selling UK property, ceasing to visit, buying an overseas burial plot etc).

Interspouse transfers

Transfers between spouses are generally free of Inheritance tax.

However, there is a special rule where one spouse is UK domiciled and the other is non UK domiciled. In this case the tax free amount is restricted to £325,000, and any amount transferred over this on death would be treated as part of the estate and potentially be subject to UK Inheritance tax.

A problem may arise where an that a UK expat goes overseas and marries. They may still retain UK property and under UK general law may well retain UK domiciliary status.

As such when they die, if they leave their assets to their spouse, the £325,000 limit could well kick in, and the value of UK property above this and the nil rate band could be subject to UK Inheritance tax.

The treaty helps to remedy this by providing for an exemption from the tax charge in the UK of up to 50 per cent on property in the estate of a deceased person who is either a national of Switzerland or is domiciled there under Article 4, which passes on death to his or her spouse domiciled outside the UK.

This is stated in Article 10:

(2) Property which passes to the spouse from a deceased person who was domiciled in or a national of Switzerland and which may be taxed in the United Kingdom shall, where:

(a) the spouse was not domiciled in the United Kingdom but the transfer would have been wholly exempt had the spouse been so domiciled, and
(b)
a greater exemption for transfers between spouses would not have been given under the law of the United Kingdom apart from this Convention, be exempt from tax in the United Kingdom to the extent of 50 per cent of the value transferred, calculated as a value on which no tax is payable and after taking account of all exemptions except those for transfers between spouses.

This could therefore cover the situation where:

'George' was a UK domiciliary but was treated as 'treaty domicile' in Switzerland. He owned significant UK property His wife was South African domicile He left the UK property to his wife on his death.
Summary

An estate tax treaty can be very beneficial, particularly as regards sorting out your domicile status. In particular the 'tiebreaker' provisions can be very useful although as always you need to ensure that you establish treaty domicile overseas as soon as possible. This would also tie in with establishing treaty residence overseas as soon as possible.

21. A REVIEW OF THE UK-US INHERITANCE TAX/ESTATE TAX TREATY

Estate tax treaties are very important in terms of mitigating inheritance tax. Although not as common as income tax treaties where they do apply they can be very effective.

In this chapter we'll run through the UK-US Estate & Gift Tax Treaty and explain how the terms apply.

ARTICLE 2
'…TAXES COVERED

(1) The existing taxes to which this Convention shall apply are:
(a) in the United States: the Federal gift tax and the Federal estate tax, including the tax on generation-skipping transfers; and
(b) in the United Kingdom: the capital transfer tax.
(2) This Convention shall also apply to any identical or substantially similar taxes which are imposed by a Contracting State after the date of signature of the Convention in addition to, or in place of, the existing taxes. The competent authorities of the Contracting States shall notify each other of any changes which have been made in their respective taxation laws…'

This is pretty self explanatory. The treaty will only apply for the US Federal gift tax and UK Inheritance tax. Although it originally applied to UK capital transfer tax it now applies to inheritance tax.

It does not apply to any US state estate tax. Any state tax suffered on overseas assets would need to be relieved under the UK's own unilateral tax credit relief.

ARTICLE 4
'…FISCAL DOMICILE
(1) For the purposes of this Convention an individual was domiciled:
(a) in the United States: if he was a resident (domiciliary) thereof or if he was a national thereof and had been a resident (domiciliary) thereof at any time during the preceding three years; and
(b) in the United Kingdom: if he was domiciled in the United Kingdom in

accordance with the law of the United Kingdom or is treated as so domiciled for the purpose of a tax which is the subject of this Convention…'

This clarifies the position in terms of domicile which is the key issue in terms of inheritance tax. You're classed as US domiciled if you're either a US resident or if you were a US citizen and had been US resident at any point in the last 3 years.

You'll be UK domicile if you're a UK domiciliary based on the usual UK rules. So you'll be looking at the domicile of origin and domicile of choice to assess where your domicile is.

You'll initially look at these rules to assess where you are classed as domicile for the purposes of the treaty. You'll then read the provisions of the treaty after taking account of your treaty domicile.

There are then specific provisions that apply if you're classed as domiciled in both the UK and the US.

Essentially these apply to direct you as domiciled in one country.

They look at which country you are a citizen of and your periods of residence.

For example if you were domiciled in both the UK and the US (ie you had a UK domicile of origin and were US resident). The treaty would class you as UK domiciled if you were a UK citizen and had not been US resident in 7 of the 10 last tax years. at that time.

If you can't assess which country is the domicile based on this rule they can then look at:

- Where you have your permanent home
- Where you have your centre of vital interests
- Where you have your habitual abode

ARTICLE 5
This where it starts to get interesting. This article looks to split up the taxing rights of the UK and US based on your treaty domicile:

'…TAXING RIGHTS

(1)(a) Subject to the provisions of Articles 6 (Immovable Property (Real Property)) and 7 (Business Property of a Permanent Establishment and Assets Pertaining to a Fixed Base Used for the Performance of Independent Personal Services) and the following paragraphs of this Article, if the decedent or transferor was domiciled in one of the Contracting States at the time of the death or transfer, property shall not be taxable in the other State.

(b) Sub-paragraph (a) shall not apply if at the time of the death or transfer the decedent or transferor was a national of that other State.

So aside from property situated abroad and business property the general rule is that assets will be taxed in the country of domicile and not in the country where the assets are located. This won't apply though if you were a national of the other country.

So for most UK resident domiciliaries with US assets any non land/non business property assets in the US would be taxed in the UK

ARTICLE 6
This applies a special rule to land and property:

'…IMMOVABLE PROPERTY
(REAL PROPERTY)

(1) Immovable property (real property) may be taxed in the Contracting State in which such property is situated.

(2) The term "immovable property" shall be defined in accordance with the law of the Contracting State in which the property in question is situated, provided always that debts secured by mortgage or otherwise shall not be regarded as immovable property. The term shall in any case include property accessory to immovable property, livestock and equipment used in agriculture and forestry, rights to which the provisions of general law respecting landed property apply, usufruct of immovable property and rights to variable or fixed payments as consideration for the working of, or the right to work, mineral deposits, sources and other natural resources; ships, boats, and aircraft shall not be regarded as

immovable property...'

So a UK domiciliary with US property would be taxed both in the UK and US on the property.

ARTICLE 7
'...BUSINESS PROPERTY OF A PERMANENT ESTABLISHMENT AND ASSETS PERTAINING TO A FIXED BASE USED FOR THE PERFORMANCE OF INDEPENDENT PERSONAL SERVICES

(1) Except for assets referred to in Article 6 (Immovable Property (Real Property)) assets forming part of the business property of a permanent establishment of an enterprise may be taxed in the Contracting State in which the permanent establishment is situated.

(2)(a) For the purposes of this Convention, the term "permanent establishment" means a fixed place of business through which the business of an enterprise is wholly or partly carried on.

(b) The term "permanent establishment" includes especially:
(i) a branch;
(ii) an office;
(iii) a factory;
(iv) a workshop; and
(v) a mine, an oil or gas well, a quarry, or any other place of extraction of natural resources.

(c) A building site or construction or installation project constitutes a permanent establishment only if it lasts for more than twelve months.

(d) Notwithstanding the preceding provisions of this paragraph, the term "permanent establishment" shall be deemed not to include:

(i) the use of facilities solely for the purpose of storage, display or delivery of goods or merchandise belonging to the enterprise;
(ii) the maintenance of a stock of goods or merchandise belonging to the enterprise solely for the purpose of storage, display or delivery;
(iii) the maintenance of a stock of goods or merchandise belonging to the enterprise

solely for the purpose of processing by another enterprise;
(iv) the maintenance of a fixed place of business solely for the purpose of purchasing goods or merchandise, or of collecting information, for the enterprise;
(v) the maintenance of a fixed place of business solely for the purpose of carrying on, for the enterprise, any other activity of a preparatory or auxiliary character; or
(vi) the maintenance of a fixed place of business solely for any combination of activities mentioned in paragraphs (i)--(v) of this sub- paragraph…

(3) Except for assets described in Article 6 (Immovable Property (Real Property)), assets pertaining to a fixed base used for the performance of independent personal services may be taxed in the Contracting State in which the fixed base is situated…'

Again, just as for land, US business property would be taxed in both the UK and US.

ARTICLE 9
If you are subject to estate/inheritance tax in both the UK and US you'll be looking at claiming a tax credit to prevent you suffering tax twice. The treaty states:

'… (a) Where the United Kingdom imposes tax with respect to property in accordance with the said Article 6 or 7, the United States shall credit against the tax calculated according to its law with respect to that property an amount equal to the tax paid in the United Kingdom with respect to that property.
(b) Where the United Kingdom imposes tax with respect to property not referred to in sub-paragraph (a) and the decedent or transferor was a national of the United States and was domiciled in the United Kingdom at the time of the death or transfer, the United States shall credit against the tax calculated according to its law with respect to that property an amount equal to the tax paid in the United Kingdom with respect to that property.

(a) Where the United States imposes tax with respect to property in accordance with the said Article 6 or 7, the United Kingdom shall credit against the tax calculated according to its law with respect to that property an amount equal to the tax paid in the United States with respect to that property.
(b) Where the United States imposes tax with respect to property not referred to in sub-paragraph (a) and the decedent or transferor was a national of the United Kingdom and was domiciled in the United States at the time of the death or

transfer, the United Kingdom shall credit against the tax calculated according to its law with respect to that property an amount equal to the tax paid in the United States with respect to that property...'

ARTICLE 10

This article looks to ensure that a UK domiciliary who is taxed in the US (eg on US property or on US business assets) is still entitled to the same reliefs and deductions that a US domiciliary would be entitled to:

'...NON-DISCRIMINATION
(1)(a) Subject to the provisions of sub-paragraph (b), nationals of a Contracting State shall not be subjected in the other State to any taxation or any requirement connected therewith which is other or more burdensome than the taxation and connected requirements to which nationals of that other State in the same circumstances are or may be subjected.
(b) Sub-paragraph (a) shall not prevent the United States from taxing a national of the United Kingdom, who is not domiciled in the United States, as a nonresident alien under its law, subject to the provisions of paragraph (5) of Article 8 (Deductions, Exemptions, Etc)...'

Conclusion

These are some of the key provisions in the treaty. Effectively the treaty provides:

- A mechanism for determining domicile for the purposes of the treaty
- That land & business property can be taxed in the country where it's located
- The country of domicile retains the right to tax the overseas asset as well
- There is a specific provision to provide a tax credit to prevent double taxation
- The non discrimination article ensures that US reliefs and exemptions can be applied in calculating any US estate tax.

22. UK TAX AND GIFTING CASH ABROAD

If you're considering gifting overseas cash to family members you should ensure that you carefully consider the UK tax implications.

A gift of cash whether in the UK or overseas is not subject to capital gains tax.

A key consideration would be inheritance tax.

If you're a non UK domiciliary you can transfer overseas cash to an overseas family member free of any UK inheritance tax charge.

However, if you're a UK domiciliary the transfer would initially be treated as a potentially exempt transfer ('PET') and subject to the 7 year requirement.

Therefore you would need to survive for 7 years after making the transfer for it to be exempt from inheritance tax.

If you're looking at transferring cash but still retaining some element of control over the use of the cash you'd need to consider whether this was treated as a 'gift with reservation of benefit'. If it was it would then remain within your estate until such time as the reservation was lifted. In order to establish whether there is a gift with reservation of benefit you would need to look at:

- Whether the recipients assumed bona fide possession and enjoyment and/or
- Whether you were entirely excluded

If either requirement is not satisfied, the gift is one with reservation.

In terms of the first requirement you would need to show that the beneficial interest in the cash had been effectively vested in the donee and that recipient(s) have had enjoyment of the gifted property. The mere legal right to enjoy it is not sufficient.

In terms of the second, again it's a question of fact whether you were entirely excluded (or virtually excluded as per the legislation).

It's fair to say that gifts of cash are less likely to fall within the reservation of benefit provisions unless you retained some express control over the cash/interest.

In some cases the giftors may look to be a signatory on the bank account. In this case you'd need to look at the legal implication of being a signatory on the account. If this meant that you were one of the legal and beneficial owners of the account it is likely that this would be classed as a reservation.

It may however be possible to arrange for a deed of gift or trust or a nominee agreement to be set up to state that you held any legal interest on behalf of the recipients (ie they held the full beneficial interest). In this case providing you did not actually benefit from the account there may be a stronger argument for no gift with reservation of benefit.

Bringing the cash into the UK

Some people ask what the tax implications of bringing the cash back into the UK are.

If you're a UK domiciliary then the cash could be brought back into the UK by the recipients without there being a UK tax charge on you. This is on the basis that you're taxed on your worldwide income and gains and therefore its likely that the overseas cash was accumulated either from post tax income or was exempt from UK tax. In either case there would be no UK tax charge on you.

If you're a non UK domiciliary and if the cash consisted of overseas income or capital gains any remittance which could benefit 'relevant people' would be classed as a remittance by you.

'Relevant people' include:

- You, the non-domiciled person

- Your spouse or civil partner
- Your partner if you're unmarried and live together as a married couple or civil partners
- Children aged under 18
- Grandchildren aged under 18

Therefore the recipients could bring the cash back without this being a remittance provided no 'relevant people' could benefit from the cash.

If any relevant people could benefit (irrespective of who the cash was actually gifted to) this would be taxed as a remittance of the income/capital gains on you.

Increases in the overseas fund

Let's assume the original gift was to children and was for £300,000. nothing were remitted for 10 years, income taxes and CGT paid on a remittance basis over this period and the value increases to £600,000. Could £300,000 be remitted tax free?

This would then be a mixed fund. Remittances would be taxed first as income, then capital gains, then tax free capital. Therefore the £300,000 could be brought back free of UK tax but only after any unremitted income/gains had been taxed first. You would still need to consider a tax charge as described above if you benefited from the remittance.

Pre owned assets charge

There can be a charge to income tax where any asset is gifted and the donee obtains a benefit. This is usually instead of the reservation of benefit provisions, and is in any case excluded where a gift falls within the reservation of benefit rules.

In terms of cash gifts though they're only caught by the pre owned asset charge if the transfer is to a settlement (as it's classed as intangible property). Therefore there is unlikely to be a pre owned asset tax charge.

23. EMIGRATING FROM THE UK TO AVOID INHERITANCE TAX

Leaving the UK to avoid inheritance tax needs to be looked at completely separately from leaving the UK to avoid income tax or capital gains tax.

The key difference is that income tax and capital gains tax are based on you losing your residence status. However, in order to avoid inheritance tax you also need to lose your domicile status.

Domicile is much wider than residence as not only does it involve losing UK residence, but it also involves severing all ties with the UK and showing an intention to live in your new country of residence permanently.

What is the benefit in terms of inheritance tax from losing UK domicile?

If you keep your UK domicile you're still within the scope of UK inheritance tax on your UK and overseas assets. This means any cash in offshore accounts or overseas properties are consolidated with your UK assets (house, car, investments etc) and are subject to inheritance tax, after UK reliefs etc have been offset.

If you manage to lose your UK domicile you will only be subject to UK inheritance tax on your UK estate. This means that your overseas assets (eg overseas properties, investments etc) will not be subject to any UK inheritance tax.

The benefit of only being taxed on your UK estate can be extended by holding UK assets via an offshore company. If you do this, you'll also be taking the UK assets held by the offshore company out of the scope of UK inheritance tax.

This is because you'll then be classed as owning shares in an offshore company as opposed to the underlying UK assets. Shares in an offshore company would be outside the scope of inheritance tax for a non UK domiciliary. Note however that changes in the 2015 Summer Budget this will not apply to UK residential property held via offshore companies in the future.

The benefits of losing UK domicile status are therefore clear. The key question is how do you lose it?

Losing UK domicile

There are two aspect to establishing an overseas domicile:

- firstly, there is a requirement to have residence in a particular country and
- secondly, they need to have an intention to live there permanently or indefinitely

This was considered in a case before the court of appeal in 2008 (Henwood v Barlow Clowes International Ltd).

In this case the judge said:

'…What has to be proved is no mere inclination arising from a passing fancy or thrust upon a man by an external but temporary pressure, but an intention freely formed to reside in a certain territory indefinitely. All the elements of the intention must be shown to exist if the change is to be established: if any one element is not proved, the case for a change fails…'

This therefore reinforces just how serious a change in domicile is. The judge stated this and said:

'…It seems to me that as a general proposition the acquisition of any new domicile should in general always be treated as a serious allegation because of its serious consequences…'

Overseas residence

One of the requirements is that you establish a residence overseas. Essentially this means that you need to establish a home overseas. Residence in this context doesn't necessarily mean tax residence but has a wider scope to include your main residence.

If you have more than one home in different countries the position is less clear and you need to look for the 'sole or chief residence.

Showing the necessary intention

The other aspect of losing domicile is to show an intention to make your new home overseas. To see exactly what the courts look at it's useful to review at the Court of Appeals decision in the Henwood case.

In this case the individual in question was trying to assert that he had lost his IOM domicile but had a new domicile of choice in Mauritius.

The judge said:

'...The principal question at trial was whether he had the necessary intention to reside there. In order to succeed on this point, Mr Henwood had to show on the balance of probabilities that it was his intention to remain there permanently or indefinitely.

The main issue with which I am concerned is whether he had the requisite intention to reside permanently or indefinitely in Mauritius. Mr Henwood had no attachment to his domicile of origin and his case is that he had left the IOM in order to start a new life. In the circumstances of this case, therefore, it is not in any way improbable that he might acquire another new domicile of choice. I remind myself that the onus of proof is on Mr Henwood.

I start with the position immediately following Mr Henwood's departure from the IOM in 1992. There can be no doubt that he would in all the circumstances have abandoned his domicile of choice there. He himself asserted that he no longer had the intention to reside there permanently or indefinitely.

The evidence was that he went to Mauritius in 1992 to take up an offer of employment (which was not long-lived) and that he leased a property on an experimental basis. It would be absurd to suggest that, immediately he left the IOM Mr Henwood acquired a domicile of choice in Mauritius.

He could only have acquired the relevant intention at some later date. Accordingly, at that point, the default rule applied and Mr Henwood's domicile was, in law, his domicile of origin…'

They then looked at his actual lifestyle both in Mauritius and elsewhere and decided that there was no subsequent intention to reside there permanently.

As the judge said:

'…So the question is whether Mr Henwood has established on a balance of probabilities that he has a domicile of choice in Mauritius. He has had a residence there for many years. But it is the quality of his residence that matters and thus he has in effect to show that he preferred Mauritius to any other place in the world.

He said that was so, but then of course these were self-serving statements. He clearly had a very comfortable and convenient residence in France. He chose to say that France was not his domicile of choice, but in my judgment, he still had to provide a satisfactory answer to this further question: if France was not his domicile of choice, what did Mauritius have for him that France did not and that clearly enabled the court to say that he had chosen to settle in Mauritius in preference to any other place where he customarily resided?

For my part, I would not accept as a reason that he liked island life. He also liked French wine and culture. I have considered the relevant factors above and none of them in my judgment provides an answer to the question I have posed. In reality, if he did not consider that France was his domicile of choice, it is unlikely that Mauritius was…'

This case reinforces just how close your ties have to be to support a change in domicile. What it does make clear though is that its just as hard to show a change in your domicile of choice as it is to show a change in from a domicile of origin to a domicile of choice.

In either case you should be looking to show very close ties with one particular jurisdiction.
Simply having a strong overseas presence in itself won't be enough.

You need to be able to fix both your residence and intention in a particular jurisdiction.

If you do have multiple homes overseas clearly establishing one as your favourite and which is your real home would therefore be advisable.

Deemed domicile

As well as losing your actual UK domicile it should be noted that you are a deemed UK domiciliary for 3 years after you actually leave the UK.

So, when you leave the UK the best you can hope for is to be outside the scope of IHT on your overseas estate after a 3 year period. In the first 3 years you would still be within the scope of UK IHT.

This assumes that you lose your UK domicile when you actually leave the UK. So, you'd need to establish your residence and intention both firmly overseas.

This would make regular UK visits etc very unlikely as this would cast doubt on your intention to live overseas.

As from April 2017, individuals who have been UK resident for more than 15 of the past 20 tax years but are foreign domiciled under general law will be deemed domiciled for all tax purposes in the UK. They will need to spend more than 5 tax years outside the UK to lose their deemed tax domicile

Where to go?

There are lots of countries that don't have any inheritance or estate taxes. China, India and Russia,Australia, Canada, Mexico, and Sweden all have no inheritance/estate tax. If you're looking at a country with low taxes generally The Isle of Man, Channel Islands, Cyprus, Malta, Gibraltar are all worth a look.

24. THE NEW £1 MILLION ALLOWANCE FOR YOUR HOME

An extra £175,000 inheritance tax allowance on the family home will be phased in from April 2017. This will combine with the original allowance of £325,000 to give some individuals a £500,000 allowance when leaving property to children and descendants on death and a combined £1m for spouses and civil partners.

The policy objective is to "[…] reduce the burden of [inheritance tax] for most families by making it easier to pass on the family home to direct descendants without a tax charge".

The "main residence nil rate band" (known as the residence nil rate band or "RNRB") will take effect from 6 April 2017
in the sum of £100,000. This sum is set to increase by £25,000 each year thereafter, stopping at £175,000 in 2020/21.

From 2021/22 onwards the band will increase in line with the Consumer Price Index.

The main residence nil rate band is available to set against the value of the deceased's property where that property is left to his/her "direct descendants" which the government has defined as a child (further defined to include a step-child, adopted child or foster child) and their lineal descendants. The allowance is restricted to property that has been the residence of the deceased at some point during their lifetime, so it would not apply to a buy-to-let property, although it could apply to a property which used to be the deceased's residence, but which was let at the date of death.

In the event that there are two potentially qualifying properties, the deceased's personal representatives can elect to which one the main residence nil rate band will attach.

Accordingly, the property to which the main residence nil rate band attaches does not have to be the deceased's principal residence either as a matter of fact or in accordance with the rules applicable to the making of a principal private residence election for capital gains tax purposes.

It would have made sense to apply this allowance to homes that qualify for principal private residence relief, although we accept that this would preclude homes that are not lived in because, for example, the owner was living in a care home. Certain periods of absence would, therefore, have to be ignored to arrive at an equitable result in line with the policy objective ora very tightly framed test for a 'family home' will need to be devised.

The Finance Act includes provisions that enable the relief to apply where a person lives in job-related accommodation and owns a house in which they "intend to live in due course".

In those circumstances, the mere fact that the individual may not, as at the date of death, have ever lived in the house in question, is not fatal to their claim. Instead, their personal representatives must establish an intention, albeit unfulfilled, to live in the house at some point in the future.

The legislation does not offer any guidance as to what evidence of the deceased's intent will be sufficient for these purposes and we will have to wait to see how this develops in practice. Aside from absences pertaining to the provision of job related accommodation, there are no other let ups.

If the value of the property in question does not utilise all of the main residence nil rate band, it will not be possible to carry across any unused allowance to another property. It is therefore important that the personal representatives elect wisely or they could potentially waste part of the allowance and face claims by those prejudiced i.e. the beneficiaries of the estate.

It is not uncommon for people to downsize to a smaller and less valuable property, or even to cease to own a property before their death. When one downsizes or ceases to own a home on or after 8 July 2015, the main residence nil rate band would still be available provided the smaller replacement property and/or the proceeds of the sale of the property (or, potentially, whatever they subsequently become) are passed to the deceased's descendants.

Quite how this will work in practice remains to be seen.

The main residence nil rate band will not be available to all, since the government does not want to be seen to be benefiting those considered to be 'better off'. The allowance will be reduced for estates worth more than £2m at a withdrawal rate of £1 for every £2 over that threshold. The £2m threshold is arrived at by deducting liabilities but before applying any applicable reliefs or exemptions (including the ordinary nil rate band, spouse/civil partner exemption, business and agricultural property reliefs etc).

The tapering of the allowance means that no relief is available for estates with a net value, in 2020/21, of £2.35m or more (or £2.7m on the death of a surviving spouse where the full main residence nil rate band is available to be transferred to the survivor -- see below).

Many people arrange their wills so that their property or a share in a property passes into a trust set up for the benefit of descendants as opposed to passing to them outright. The legislation states that the main residence nil rate band will apply to certain types of trust only.

These include trusts where the descendant is treated as if they own the property themselves (e.g. a qualifying life interest), and trusts for minor descendants and those under the age of 25.

Accordingly, if a discretionary trust is used, the allowance will be lost.

Where someone leaves everything they own to a surviving spouse or civil partner, the value of the estate inherited is fully exempt from inheritance tax by virtue of spouse or civil partner exemption.

This means that the first to die has not used any of their own nil rate band and, since October 2007, the unused proportion of their nil rate band is available to transfer or, more accurately, increase the nil rate band of the second spouse or civil partner when they die.

Like the original nil rate band, the main residence nil rate band will be transferable between spouses and civil partners where the second spouse or civil partner dies on or after 6 April 2017 irrespective of when the first spouse dies. For example, if the second death occurs in the 2020/21 tax year, a husband and wife can combine their nil rate bands making a combined allowance of £1m made up of two original nil rate bands of £350,000 (£650,000) and two main residence nil rate bands of £175,000 (£350,000).

Some tips and traps

1. The RNRB only applies to transfers on death, not during lifetime

Consequently it will not apply to lifetime gifts when the donor dies within seven years. However, the RNRB will be available for property treated as being part of the deceased's estate because he has made a lifetime gift but retained some benefit from the gifted property.

2. The property does not need to be left by will

The RNRB may also apply on intestacy or where joint property passes by survivorship.

3. It is not necessary for the property to have been the deceased's main residence (or his residence at the time of his death)

Instead, it is sufficient that it has been used as his residence at some point during his ownership.

4. The RNRB is only available in relation to one property

If the deceased had more than one residence, his personal representatives can nominate which is to benefit from the RNRB.

5. 'Direct descendant' is defined widely

It includes stepchild, adopted child and foster child. It also includes the spouse or civil partner, or a widow/widower or surviving civil partner who has not remarried, of a direct descendant.

6. Certain trusts for direct descendants will not qualify for the RNRB

If a property is left on trust for direct descendants, the RNRB will be available only in limited circumstances, for example where they have a right to trust income, or the property is left on particular favoured trusts for children, or on a disabled person's trust. No RNRB will be available for trusts outside these limited exceptions, such as discretionary trusts or trusts for grandchildren who do not receive the property outright on the deceased's death, unless it is possible to use a deed of variation or trust appointment to 're-write' the trust terms.

7. The RNRB may also be available if the deceased was a trust beneficiary

The allowance may be available in certain circumstances where a deceased had a right to use a property held in trust and on his death someone receives the property outright.

8. The RNRB will be tapered away for estates over £2m

As a result in 2017/18, an estate over £2.2m will not benefit from the RNRB at all. When the relief reaches £175,000 in 2020/21, the cut-off will apply to estates over £2.35m.

9. Unused RNRB may be transferred to a surviving spouse or civil partner even if the first to die did not own a residence

However, where the first death occurs before 6 April 2017, the transferred RNRB is limited to £100,000.

10. The RNRB may still be available if the individual has downsized.

Finance Act 2016 legislation extends the availability of the RNRB to those who downsize (or cease to own a home) after on or after 8 July 2015, provided that their direct descendants are left some of their estate outright or on permitted trusts.

Planning points

The value of an estate should be kept under review in light of the taper threshold of £2m. Remember that, for this purpose, the value of the estate is calculated net of debts, but any reliefs or exemptions are not deducted.

Avoid 'bunching' of a couple's estates where this will mean that the taper threshold is exceeded on the second death. In such a case consider leaving property on trust for the survivor (instead of direct to them). Take care that a mortgage does not reduce the net value of a home below the amount of the available RNRB.

If a residence is to be left on trust for direct descendants, the trust terms must be considered carefully to ensure that the RNRB will be available.

Those who wish to rely on the downsizing rules will need to keep careful records of the proceeds of sale (or of the property value at the date of a gift) so that the 'lost' RNRB may be ascertained at the relevant time.

Summary

Although the introduction of the RNRB is good news for taxpayers, its scope is fairly restricted. In particular, the fact that it will only be available to those who leave a residence to direct descendants and the application of the taper threshold for estates over £2m will mean that it has limited relevance for some taxpayers. However, as the government has confirmed that the NRB will be frozen at £325,000 until at least 5 April 2021, it will be important for individuals to take advantage of this new relief where it is available to them. Such individuals should carry out a careful review of the organisation of their estates and the terms of their wills, especially where a residence is to be left in trust, to ensure that they gain the maximum benefit from the RNRB.

25. NON DOMS AND UK RESIDENTIAL PROPERTY AFTER APRIL 2017

From April 2017, all UK residential property held by a non UK domiciliary ("non-dom"), whether directly or indirectly, including UK residential property held by offshore companies, offshore trust and company structures and non-UK partnerships will be subject to UK inheritance tax.

Currently, UK assets held by a non-dom (or a trust set up by a nondom) indirectly through, for example, a non-UK company are not subject to UK inheritance tax.

The changes will affect all UK residential property of any value whether it is owner occupied or let. They will not, however, bring other UK assets held indirectly by non-doms (through, for example, a non-UK company) within the charge to UK inheritance tax.

These changes mean, for example, that:

- where a non-dom gifts the shares in a non-UK company which holds UK residential property to a trust an immediate charge to inheritance tax will arise;
- a charge to inheritance tax will arise on the 10 year anniverasry of a trust set up by a non-dom which holds UK residential property through a non-UK company;
- a charge to inheritance tax will arise on the death of a nondom who owns shares in a non-UK company which holds UK residential property;
- where a non-dom gifts the shares in a non-UK company which holds UK residential property to another individual no charge to inheritance tax will arise if the non-dom survives the gift by seven years.

The past two tax years have seen the introduction of ATED, ATED related capital gains tax and non-resident capital gains tax (where this is also relevant).

If such individuals have purchased residential property through a corporate structure, they may also have suffered stamp duty land tax at the higher rate where the property was valued at more than £2 million -- or more recently, more than £500,000. The one tax advantage of holding residential property through a corporate structure that remained was the shelter provided from inheritance tax; but now this too is being withdrawn.

For some individuals, the non-tax advantages of holding property through a structure may still outweigh the tax disadvantages. These include confidentiality of ownership and asset protection, and the potential avoidance of forced heirship rules, whether Sharia or civil law based.

One key non-tax advantage of holding property through a structure is the avoidance of the need for UK probate on the death of an individual where the property owned is shares in an offshore company, rather than the underlying UK property. This may no longer apply from April 2017 if a grant of probate in some form is required, albeit possibly in relation to the shares in the company.

These changes mean that many non-doms who chose not to 'deenvelope' despite the introduction (and increase in) the Annual Tax on Enveloped Dwellings (which was introduced from April 2013) to preserve the inheritance tax advantages of hold UK residential property through a non-UK company may now feel there is no benefit in retaining the company and will wish to de-envelope.

However, de-enveloping now could potentially give rise to significant costs which would not have been as great had the property been deenveloped earlier.

Diversely-held vehicles that hold UK residential property will not be subject to the new inheritance tax charge.

Non-UK assets held by a non-dom and non-UK assets held within a trust established by a non-dom (and not deemed domiciled individual) will remain outside the charge to UK inheritance tax.

Lower-value properties held directly may fall within a couple's joint nil rate bands. This is currently £325,000 each or £650,000 jointly. However, as we've seen in the previous chapter an additional nil rate band will be available for property used as a main residence passed on death to direct descendants. This will start in tax year 2017/2018 (increasing from £100,000 initially to £175,000 in 2020/2021) and any unused nil rate band will be available to be transferred to a surviving spouse or civil partner who dies on or after April 6 2017, regardless of when the first death occurred.

There will be a tapered withdrawal of the additional nil rate band for estates with a net value of more than £2 million, at a rate of £1 for every £2 over this threshold.

However, no additional inheritance tax mitigation may be necessary if there are no other significant UK assets and the net value threshold applies only to property within an individual's taxable estate under the new rules when they are introduced.

Alternatively, property may be purchased with a mortgage to reduce its value in a non-domiciled individual's estate. Legislation introduced in 2013, which restricts the deductibility of liabilities for inheritance tax purposes in certain circumstances, may limit the effectiveness of such a strategy where the relevant legislation applies.

For an individual wishing to invest in UK residential property generally rather than in any specific property, investing in a diversely held fund or non-resident company that invests in such property may be an alternative tax-efficient option, as it appears that the new provisions will not apply to diversely held entities.

It is also worth bearing in mind that UK commercial real estate held within an offshore structure will not be caught by the new inheritance tax rules under the proposals; nor will other forms of UK situate non-residential property or foreign property.

26. HOW SHAREHOLERS CAN USE CROSS OPTIONS TO RETAIN BUSINESS PROPERTY RELIEF

The death of a shareholder who is also a director can have a major impact on any business, particularly where the company has not made plans for such an event. For owner/managers of small to medium-sized private companies, this is a particular concern, since the shareholder's death can potentially give rise to a host of adverse consequences for the business.

Shareholders may also have concerns for the welfare of the beneficiaries in the event of death. When a shareholder dies, his beneficiaries' interests do not necessarily align with those of the other shareholders, especially where such beneficiaries lack any business experience. As the company is under no obligation to provide a deceased shareholder's beneficiaries with benefits such as income or pensions, it is clear that such concerns are entirely legitimate. Regardless of assurances a shareholder may give his fellow shareholder that he will make sure that his fellow shareholder's wife and children are 'looked after' in the event of death, if the shareholders have not made formal provisions, the worst case scenario can, and sometimes does, happen.

In such circumstances, the question of whether the continuing shareholders have sufficient funds to buy the deceased's shares becomes critical. In many cases, a suitably-drafted cross-option agreement, backed by an appropriate term assurance policy is the solution. This can be drafted on a stand-alone basis or can be included as a separate section in a shareholders' agreement.

The fundamentals of a cross-option agreement are simple: each shareholder agrees that upon his death his fellow shareholders have the option to buy his shares (and, in some cases, those of his spouse), usually at market value (a so-called 'call option') and that his personal representatives (on death) have the option to sell his shares (and, in some cases, those of his spouse) to the continuing shareholders (a 'put option').

At the same time, each shareholder takes out a term assurance policy, under which any amount which becomes payable under the policy is held in trust by the continuing shareholders to pay for the deceased's shares under the put and call options.

By structuring the transfer of shares in this way it is possible to ensure that the deceased's shares qualify for business property relief (which, in valid circumstances, provides 100% relief from inheritance tax) whilst the proceeds of the insurance policy fall outside of the deceased's estate and are not subject to inheritance tax.

It is essential that the person drafting the cross-option agreement appreciates the necessity to ensure that it does not fall foul of certain inheritance tax provisions, which could render the transfer of the shares ineligible for business property relief. The key factor is that the ability for the continuing shareholders to buy the deceased's shares and the ability for the deceased's personal representatives to sell the shares must be drafted as a right, rather than an obligation. If any of the parties is under an obligation to buy or sell the deceased's shares, the transfer of the shares would effectively be subject to a binding contract for sale and, as such, for inheritance tax purposes would be treated as a transfer of cash and, consequently, business property relief would be lost.

A properly-drafted cross-option agreement with associated term policies not only ensures that a deceased shareholder's beneficiaries can extract value from the company, but it does so in a way which is both tax-efficient and causes minimum disruption to the remaining shareholders.

27. HOW TO GIVE AWAY PROPERTY FOR IHT PURPOSES BUT STILL LIVE THERE

One of the major problem areas in inheritance tax (IHT) planning is the family residence. How can the taxpayer give it away and continue living there?

The answer lies in FA 1986 s102B(4).

Billy and his Father

Let us assume that Peat Manor is owned by the father (F) of Billy (B) and he lives in the same. He is aged 75 years and in good health. B is in his early 30s. He has a flat in London and is there for the working days of the week. F gifts a 50% share of Peat Manor to B and he continues to pay for the upkeep of the property. After the gift the two would occupy the Peat Manor albeit B has and continues to use his London flat.

THE RELIEVING SECTION

The gift of the undivided share in Peat Manor to B will avoid the gift with reservation of benefit (GROB) provisions if:

• the donor and donee occupy the land

• the donor does not receive any benefit, other than a negligible one, which is provided by or at the expense of the donee for some reason connected with the gift.

This provision has effect from 9/3/1999, and the position prior thereto was governed by a Hansard Statement.

HMRC refer to the legislation setting "out in statutory form the practice which had already been adopted" but the two do differ in certain respects as dealt with below.

ANALYSING THE SECTION

Occupation

Under the proposal the two will occupy the house even though B may only spend weekends or most weekends there and some holidays. B will leave possessions at the property and has his own bedroom, and it is open to him at all times. With regard to his London flat he should consider TCGA 1992 s222 (5).

There is no clear HMRC guidance here, but HMRC give a wide meaning to occupation in the pre-owned assets tax (POAT) provisions in FA 2004 Sch 15. Storage and a right to use with minimal actual occupation may well constitute occupation for those purposes.

If the taxpayer has the right to occupy the premises as a 50% owner in common, treats it as his home, is physically present there most weekends and for some holidays, has an earmarked bedroom and study, keeps some of his possessions there and has the keys to come and go as he pleases, and he is not just a guest or temporary visitor, he is in occupation for the purposes of s.102B(4).

There should be no problems in F living in part only of Peat Manor and B doing the same. F may occupy an entire house, although his son B has his own room and study. F can enter the rooms as he pleases and store things there, and he may go into the rooms to hear music or for some quiet when B is out, or to chat to B when he is there. They both occupy the rooms. The old Hansard statement limited the relief to occupation as a "family home." That is not a requirement of the legislation.

If the donee gives up occupation

If B gives up occupation after the proposal has been implemented the property falls back into the estate of F for IHT purposes.

Note that if F (and B) sell the property, 50% will belong to B, and the full CGT residence relief will not be available on B's share. B must consider his capital gains tax (CGT) position as he has two main residences.

Note because F is caught by the GROB rules POAT is not in issue (see FA 2004 Sched 15 para.11(5)(a)).

No benefit to be provided at the expense of the donee

This is an odd requirement. B must not overpay for his use of the property. Indeed the safest course is for F to pay all the running costs -- council tax bill, gas and electricity, cleaning, TV licence, maintenance -- and the capital outlays also. The capital outlays may be gifts in themselves (of those capital outlays as to 50%), sending another seven years running with respect to those outlays. But little turns on that: the main prize is to take -- say -- half of the property out of charge after seven years.

The HMRC manual refers to the need for both parties to "share the outgoings", but what they have in mind is B not bearing all the outgoings or more than his share of the same.

Under the old statement, the sharing of outgoings was envisaged, and also each person enjoying a separate part of the house; neither points are relevant to the statutory requirements.

There must be a gift

F must do a deed of gift in favour of B. The gift will be a potentially exempt transfer within IHTA 1984 s 3A.

Note in calculating the fall in value the part retained is discounted to reflect the fact of joint ownership. On F's death this discount is reflected in the value of his estate, reducing the IHT payable on his death on the share retained: a half of a house is worth less than 50% of the total value of the house.

Undivided Share

The gift should be of a tenancy in common interest.

Pre owned asset tax (POAT)

Generally the proposal is within the ambit of POAT, but there is an exclusion in FA 2004 Schedule 15 paragraph 11(5)(c), if the property interest given to the son "would fall to be treated as property which is subject to a reservation of benefit" but for s.102B(4).

28. WHEN THE 7 YEAR INHERITANCE TAX SURVIVORSHIP PERIOD CAN BE AVOIDED

There are a number of key options or exemptions that allow transfers to be made which aren't classed as 'potentially exempt transfers' ('PET's'). If they're not PETS they won't then be subject to the 7 year survivorship period.

This article takes a quick look at some of these options:

Annual exemption

Everyone has an annual exemption of £3,000 per tax year. If the previous years exemption is unused this can be brought forward to provide for a maximum relief of £6,000 in the current year. Where possible you should ensure that this is utilised.

Marriage exemption

There is a bonus exemption of £5,000 for children and £2,500 for other close relatives.

Normal expenditure out of income

An inheritance tax exemption that is often overlooked is the exemption for 'normal expenditure out of income'. Where this applies it can lead to amounts paid to family/relative/a trust to be excluded from a deceased's estate when calculating any inheritance tax charge.

In order for payments under the normal expenditure out of income exemption to be exempt, the following conditions must be satisfied:

- the transfer must be made as part of the normal expenditure of the transferor
- it must be made out of his income

- after allowing for all transfers forming part of his normal expenditure, the transferor was left with sufficient income to maintain his usual standard of living.

All three conditions must be satisfied and the onus is on the tax payer to show that they are all satisfied. HMRC accept that it could be that only part of a transfer actually meets the conditions and you'd therefore have a situation where part of a gift was excluded from the estate and the remainder was included.

'Normal expenditure' means that based on the particular transferor, the payment was typical for them. Ideally a regular pattern of payments should be made, or an agreed percentage (eg 10%) of net income would need to be shown to be paid to the recipients.

One way that expenditure could be classed as 'normal' would be for an individual to have assumed a commitment or adopted a firm resolution regarding his future expenditure and thereafter complied with it. There would therefore need to be evidence supporting the regular payments. This could be a simple family agreement indicating payments to be made by (for example) a father to his children.

A common example is where a specific payment is to be made monthly or annually. This could be (for example) payments of £2,808 per tax year into a stakeholder pension for the benefit of a child.

If a regular cash transfer is to be made to a child, a good option would be to consider making any payments under a deed of covenant. This would be likely to satisfy HMRC that a pattern of expenditure will be in place.

In essence the final condition above relates to whether the deceased would have sufficient income to live on after making the transfers in question. His usual standard of living is taken to generally be the standard prevailing at the time of the transfer.

HMRC could therefore look to see details of the net income of the deceased and compare this with the usual costs of living they incur.

This can however be a useful way to transfer significant sums over a few tax years without being caught by the 7 year rule.

Business assets

If you invested cash into assets that qualified for full business property relief ('BPR') this could be exempt from inheritance tax on your death.

Typical assets that would qualify include shares in an unquoted trading company and an investment into your trading partnership or other trading business.

One of the most common investments here would be investments into EIS shares. The downside is the increased but from an inheritance tax perspective they could be very attractive.

Note that there is a two year ownership period to qualify for the inheritance tax exemption. Therefore rather than 7 years you'd need to survive for 2 years.

It's worthwhile noting that tenanted businesses won't qualify for 100% relief. So if for example you owned a property that was let to a trading business it wouldn't qualify for business property relief.

29. DEBTS ON DEATH AND IHT PLANNING

On death, IHT is chargeable on your "net" estate; essentially, what you own at your death less what you owe at your death.

The only post death expense that's allowable for IHT is the funeral account plus a reasonable amount for mourning expenses, say a wake or post funeral reception.

The debt must be real and truly repayable; signing an IOU in favour of your son for £1million when he's not actually loaned you any money won't work. HMRC will look very carefully at debts owed to close friends and family and will need evidence of a written or verbal agreement to repay, and evidence that the deceased was, or would be, making repayments.

Similarly, a debt legally due, but, in truth, unlikely ever to be called in or repaid, won't be allowable.

Otherwise, it's the purpose for which the money was borrowed that's important, rather than the property given as security for the loan. Your house might have been given as security for a bank loan, but the debt to the bank won't be allowable for IHT if the money was spent on IHT-free assets (for example farmland or business assets or an AIM portfolio).

It remains possible to borrow money and to give that money away. If you survive the gift by seven years, the debt remains allowable for IHT purposes, and the borrowed money given away will have fallen out of account. Parents with valuable property but limited liquid assets often will take out a lifetime mortgage or equity release to realise a cash sum from their property and then gift the cash to their children or grandchildren. But do the maths. The compounding of interest on, say, an "equity release" loan will substantially reduce the overall saving. And if you die within seven years, such that the value given is retrospectively chargeable to IHT, there may be no saving at all.

Persons domiciled outside the UK pay IHT only on their UK assets. So if they own nothing in the UK apart from, say, a house, it's best they borrow as much of the purchase price as possible. The debt will reduce the value of the asset for IHT purposes. It matters not that they had sufficient resources to buy the house without recourse to borrowing.

With traditional, IHT-efficient structures for non- domiciled persons buying UK property (usually though an offshore company within an offshore trust) likely to be ineffective for IHT from April 2017 after legislative changes, many will fall back on the simple process of borrowing all, or a large part, of the purchase monies.

Remember, only monies borrowed by the non-domiciliary to buy the property will normally be allowable. Borrowing money secured on the property at a later date and investing the borrowed money in overseas assets, outside the IHT net, won't work.

Of course, just as you might owe monies on your death, so too might you be owed monies. The amount of any debt due to you will be chargeable to IHT. But that doesn't stop your executors arguing that all or part of the monies due should be discounted for IHT purposes if there's little or no likelihood of repayment . The borrower may have gone bankrupt, say, or proved to be a "man of straw", with no chance of ever being in a position to repay.

30. WHEN IS IT WORTH FORMING A LIFETIME TRUST FOR UK TAX PLANNING AND HOW TO DETERMINE WHICH TYPE OF TRUST TO USE

Most trusts are now classed as relevant property trusts and as such are subject to 10 year and exit charges.

Tax disincentives of creating new lifetime trusts

There are significant tax disincentives in making a transfer of non excluded property upon lifetime trusts including:

(1) The transfer to the trust gives rise to IHT, with an immediate charge at 20% above the settlor's unused nil rate band, even if the settlor survives for 7 years .

(2) Although a gain on the disposal of assets into the trust can be held over, being a disposal which is a chargeable transfer for IHT purposes such relief is not available if the settlement is "settlor interested".

This will be the case if the settlor, spouse or civil partner of the settlor, or a dependent child has an interest under the trust.

A dependent child means a child who is under the age of 18, unmarried, and does not have a civil partner

(3) The trust will be subject to 10-year anniversary and exit charges.

(4) On the termination of a post-21 March 2006 IIP for another individual absolutely, there will not be a PET, but there will be an exit charge.

(5) The tax-free uplift on death, for assets subject to CGT, will not apply to the trust assets, whereas it would have applied to those assets had they been retained as part of the settlor's free estate.

Is it better to make an outright gift?

In many cases, it would be more tax effective for a potential settlor to make an outright gift to another individual or individuals, or to a bare trust for an individual, including a minor:

(1) The gift will qualify as a PET.

(2) There will be no 10 year anniversary and exit charges.

(3) If there is a gain, it cannot be held over. But that is also the case where there is a disposal to a settlor - interested trust (as widely defined). It may in any event be possible to gift assets which are not pregnant with gain, or to give cash.

(4) The donee (unless a minor) can make a PET of the gifted property in due course in the hope of surviving for 7 years.

(5) The CGT - free uplift, on the death of the donee, will apply to assets retained by the donee at death.

Consequences for use of lifetime trusts

In many cases, a potential settlor will not want to make an outright gift to an individual, or to a bare trust for a minor.

The settlor may want the flexibility of a trust under which discretionary powers are given to the trustees; or to limit the interest of a beneficiary, e.g. to income; or to postpone entitlement beyond the age of 18.

However, the biggest disincentive to the use of a lifetime trust is that the settlement of sums in excess of the nil rate band (currently £325,000) is subject to an immediate charge at 20% on the value transferred above the nil rate band. Therefore, most new lifetime trusts will:

a. be of a value limited to the settlor's nil rate band (currently £325,000);

b. comprise property attracting business or agricultural property relief;

c. be of "excluded property"; or

d. fall within the normal expenditure out of income exemption.

Excluded property

Property held in a trust is excluded property if the settlor was domiciled outside the U.K. when he made the settlement, and the trust property is not situated in the U.K.

Trusts of foreign property settled by a non U.K. domiciled settlor have certain advantages provided that the trust continues to hold foreign property:

(1) The transfer by a non U.K. domiciled settlor of foreign property into a trust during his lifetime will not give rise to a transfer of value for IHT purposes.

(2) If the foreign property is settled by the will of a non U.K. domiciled person, there will be no IHT charge on the death of the testator in respect of that foreign property since a person's estate immediately before death does not include excluded property.

(3) The settlor can retain an interest in a lifetime trust until death. Even though the trust property will be property subject to a reservation of benefit on death, such property will be excluded property outside the charge to IHT. If, before the death of the settlor, the foreign property ceases to be subject to a reservation of benefit, the settlor will be deemed not to have made a transfer of value.

(4) The trust will not be subject to exit and 10 year charges. A distribution to a U.K. beneficiary will not, therefore, be subject to an exit charge.

Using a Discretionary trust or Life interest trust?

For IHT purposes, the form of a lifetime trust does not much matter, since all trusts, other than disabled person's trusts, will be subject to the relevant property regime. Normally, a full discretionary trust is used for maximum flexibility.

However, an IIP trust, such as a life interest trust, may have some attractions, even if such a trust is within the relevant property regime for IHT purposes:

(1) The settlor may want to ensure that, say, a spouse, is entitled to income for life, and/or that other beneficiaries, such as the settlor's children, are entitled to capital on the death of the life tenant.

(2) A higher special rate of income tax (currently 37.5% on dividend income, and 45% on other income) is payable by the trustees of a discretionary or A&M trust. In the case of an IIP trust, the income can be mandated to the beneficiary, who will pay income tax at his or her rates. The trustees will not need to submit a tax return.

(3) It is possible, if desired, to introduce great flexibility in the case of a life interest trust, by giving the trustees overriding powers of appointment and extended powers of advancement.

Flexible IIP trust for grandchildren

A trust could, therefore, be created whereby:

(a) The income of the trust fund is payable to the settlor's first grandchild for life.

(b) If another grandchild is born, the trustees can appoint one half of the trust fund to the second grandchild. This would not give rise to a transfer of value, as the trust would still be wholly within the relevant property regime.

(c) On the death of a grandchild with an IIP, no charge would arise so long as that grandchild's interest remained settled

31. IHT PLANNING FOR JOINT ACCOUNTS

Joint bank accounts may be a flexible and practical solution for the management of money on a day to day basis. Many couples have joint accounts to make paying bills and arranging household finances easier.

It is not uncommon for elderly parents to ask one of their children to become a joint signatory on their bank account, to assist them in operating the account as they get older.

However, joint accounts can present several problems if one of the account holders dies. These include quantifying the extent of the deceased's share of the funds, identifying who is entitled to receive those funds and ascertaining the inheritance tax treatment.

Succession issues

Normally, the balance in a joint account will pass to the surviving account holder on death by right of survivorship, outside the terms of the deceased's Will. This is because almost all joint accounts will be held as "joint tenants" rather than as "tenants in common". Consequently, there is often no need to wait for probate; the survivor will simply provide the death certificate to the bank and it will transfer the money into the survivor's sole name.

The normal mandate on a joint bank account provides for this and enables either of the named parties to withdraw the whole amount for his own benefit while they are both alive. However, although this may be the starting position as regards the account holders and the bank, the parties' rights as against each other may depend on what else they have agreed and the purpose for which the account was opened and how it has been operated.

The true position may require careful consideration. This can be a difficult job of piecing together the facts and circumstances, occasionally involving acrimony, as there is usually no written evidence to clarify the position. Joint accounts are often run on the basis of an informal mutual understanding between the account holders but once one of them dies, that may be difficult to ascertain.

This was demonstrated in the case of Drakeford v Cotton and Stain, where an elderly mother set up and fully funded a joint bank account with one of her daughters. It was agreed that when the joint account was established, the deceased had not intended to give her daughter a beneficial interest. However, over time, the mother's intentions changed since she made it clear to the daughter and to her son that the daughter should inherit the account after her death. The court came to this conclusion on a review of the surrounding circumstances including evidence that the mother had fallen out with her other daughter, and wished to disinherit her.

There is a long line of cases on joint bank accounts with a variety of different outcomes as each turns on its own facts. The parties' intentions are key but ideally the position should be properly documented.

Inheritance tax issues

Joint accounts are common between spouses and civil partners. While they are both alive, interest from a joint bank account is normally taxed 50/50 as they are treated as owning the funds in equal shares. If the funds are owned in unequal shares, they will still be taxed on the 50/50 basis unless they make a joint declaration to be taxed according to their beneficial interests.

Other joint account holders will usually hold the funds as "joint tenants" and will also be taxed equally on the income unless in fact they hold the funds unequally as "tenants in common", in which case they will be subject to income tax on their share of the interest.

HMRC pays close attention to joint accounts after a death, particularly if there is a significant amount of tax at stake. They are not greatly interested in joint accounts held by spouses and civil partners where funds passing from one spouse or civil partner to the other are normally 100% exempt from inheritance tax.

However, for unmarried couples and other combinations of joint account holders, a greater degree of scrutiny will be required as to how much tax is due and who is liable for that tax. It can not be assumed that the deceased will be treated as owning 50% of the funds and that inheritance tax will only apply to that half share. Similarly, it can not be assumed that any inheritance tax due will be paid from the deceased's general estate; more often it will be payable by the surviving joint account holder if they inherit the funds by survivorship.

The Inheritance Tax Return that must be submitted after a death calls for a surprising amount of detail including:

- the name of the other account holder and their relationship to the deceased;
- the date on which the joint ownership began;
- the amount provided by each joint owner;
- how any income from the account was dealt with;
- withdrawals from the joint account.

HMRC will normally regard each account holder as beneficially entitled to the proportion of the account attributable to their contributions. So, if the deceased provided all the money, the whole amount will be subject to inheritance tax on his death. The reservation of benefit rules are in point where a person places funds in a joint account with someone else and either receives all the interest or has the right to withdraw all the money (as is normally the case). Withdrawals generally count against each party's contributions but where there is a lot of activity on an account, it may be extremely difficult to unravel the movements.

Any withdrawals in excess of the funds provided by each joint owner will potentially constitute a gift to the other party. This in itself has inheritance tax consequences and may also be relevant for income tax purposes.

Another case, Pflum v HMRC, concerned the question of whether withdrawals from a joint bank account were taxable remittances. An account which was funded entirely by a non-domiciled UK resident was drawn on by his girlfriend in the UK. It was held that the withdrawals became the property of the girlfriend and at the time these were not taxable remittances by him.

However, since Finance Act 2008, the boyfriend would now be taxable on his girlfriend's withdrawals under the same set of circumstances as she would be a 'relevant person' in relation to him.

These cases serve as a reminder of some of the issues to be aware of with joint accounts, where the position may be more complicated than it first appears.

32. HOW TO USE A NIL RATE BAND "SETTLOR INTERESTED TRUST" TAX EFFICIENTLY

Settlor interested trusts are typically not used by the well advised for a number of very good reasons:

(1) So as to avoid a gift with a reservation of benefit to the settlor for IHT purposes.

If a benefit is reserved to the settlor in settled property on the settlor's death, the settled property will be deemed to form part of the settlor's estate.

(2)Because the gain on a disposal to a settlor-interested trust cannot be held over. A settlor-interested trust includes a settlement in which any property is or will or may become payable to or applicable for the benefit of the settlor or his spouse or civil partner, or a child of the settlor at a time when the child is a dependent child of his.

A dependent child means a child or stepchild who is under the age of 18 years, unmarried, and does not have a civil partner.

(3) So as to avoid the income of the settlement being charged to the settlor, which will be the case where the settlor, the settlor's spouse or civil partner has an interest in settled property, except in limited permitted circumstances. The income is taxed at the highest part of the settlor's income.

(4) So as to avoid a pre-owned assets (POAT) charge which can arise where a settlor disposes of an interest in land, which he occupies, or chattels of which he has possession or use; or where he has an interest in a settlement of intangible property (not land or chattels). However, there is no POAT charge if the settlor has reserved a benefit for IHT purposes.

What this means is that for anyone considering using a Settlor-Interested trust:

(a) The transfer by the settlor into the trust will be immediately chargeable at 20% above the nil rate band, rising to a maximum of 40% on a death within 3 - 7 years.

(b) There will be a reservation of benefit for IHT purposes with the result that the trust property will form part of the settlor's estate on his death if the settlor continues to reserve a benefit until death.

(c) The trust will be subject to 10-year charges and exit charges.

(d) Hold-over relief will not be available on any gain arising on the disposal by the settlor of assets into the trust.

(e) The income of the trust will be taxed as the settlor's income.

(f) There will be no CGT-free uplift on the settlor's death.

Given all of this, it's no surprise that Settlor-Interested trusts aren't typically used.

However in spite of this a self-settlement of the nil rate band may have tax advantages.

Example: Self-settlement of the nil-rate band

Jack has made no chargeable transfers within the last 7 years.

He settles £325,000 in cash on a life interest trust for himself, remainder to his children, but with no power to advance capital to him.

The trustees invest in a buy-to-let property which produces an income for Jack.

The tax analysis is:

(a) The transfer into the trust gives rise to no IHT liability, being within the nil rate band.

(b) After 7 years the transfer will not form part of Jack's cumulative total for IHT purposes.

(c) There is no gift with a reservation of benefit by Jack: he has given away a deferred right to capital, and retained a right to income.

Jack will have carved out an interest, i.e. an interest in income for his life. He will have made a gift of the capital subject to his retained life interest, rather than giving away the whole beneficial interest and reserving a benefit out of what he has given away.

(d) There will be no reservation of benefit under Finance Act 1986, s. 102A which would arise if Jack had made a gift of an interest in land, and he or his spouse or civil partner enjoyed a significant right or interest, or is party to a significant arrangement which entitles or enables Jack to occupy all or part of the land, or to enjoy some right in relation to all or part of the land, otherwise than for full consideration in money or money's worth.

The gift will not be of land, but of cash.

(e) On Jack's death his life interest will not be included as an asset in his estate as it arose after 22 March 2006. However, there will not be a tax-free uplift on his death. A CGT charge will arise if a beneficiary becomes absolutely entitled.

(f) 10-year and exit charges will be avoided if and so long as the trust remains a nil rate band trust.

(g) There is no CGT charge on the disposal of cash into the settlement.

(h) There is no POAT charge as that charge would only arise if Jack were in occupation of the property (which he will not be); or if the trust property is intangible property, other than land or chattels (which it is not: it is land).

(i) The income will be taxed as Jack's income (but Jack receives the income anyway).

Jack can, in this way, retain a right to income for life, but avoid IHT on the trust assets if he survives for 7 years.

ABOUT THE AUTHOR

Lee Hadnum LLB ACA CTA is an international tax specialist. He is a Chartered Accountant and Chartered Tax Adviser and is the Editor of the popular tax planning website:

www.wealthprotectionreport.co.uk

Lee is also the author of a number of best selling tax planning books.

19773081R00076

Printed in Poland
by Amazon Fulfillment
Poland Sp. z o.o., Wrocław